ESS

"If you're r   n your life, *fearLESS* is the best place to start. I've never read a book about working through the mindset issues that block our happiness and success that's as packed with hands-on, step-by-step information as this one. *fearLESS* is a smart and expertly-written book that will empower your life. Read it once, then read it again with a pen, highlighter, and sticky notes because you'll (finally) know *exactly* what to do and how to do it to create lasting success both at work and at home."

~DAVID NEWMAN, AUTHOR OF *DO IT! MARKETING* | WWW.DOITMARKETING.COM

"*fearLESS* is a treasure trove of easy-to-implement strategies that will have you reaching *through* your fears and conquering your dreams on the other side. Nathalie Thompson's wisdom and understanding, coupled with her concrete explanations and exercises make her the expert guide for anyone wanting to achieve more, now. In short: Got dreams? Get *fearLESS*."

~ KATHY PFEIFFER, CEO, BEAUTYVALUED.COM

"If you're READY to kick Fear to the curb and become fearless in every area of your life, Thompson's book is a must. Unlocking the causes of fear and shifting the faulty perceptions that block your success is a freedom worth achieving! Everything you want is waiting for you, on the other side of fear, and *fearLESS* will help get you there faster... then you can truly live your life by design."

~ KELLY FIDEL, SPEAKER, CEO, NO GLASS CEILING™ | WWW.NOGLASSCEILING.COM

"Anyone with a dream in their heart -- and that's everyone -- struggles with self-doubt, wondering at times: "Am I good enough to succeed?" Thompson really walks the talk, avoiding fluffy platitudes and skillfully navigating the reader through the mental minefield of insecurity by offering a tempered, step-by-step, guide to slaying the dragons of real and imagined fears that suppress the greatness that lies within each of us. *fearLESS* is a terrific roadmap to following your heart and following your dreams. Everyone should read this book."

~SEUMAS GALLACHER, AUTHOR OF THE JACK CALDER CRIME SERIES | WWW.SEUMASGALLACHER.COM

"The title says it all! But how the hell can you practice that when you're still in the fear? I picked up this book when I was having a truly rough week and it was exactly what I needed to connect back in to the powerful me I'd forgotten about. Thanks, Nathalie, for writing a book that takes a short cut right into the heart of the matter...and uplifts instantly! *fearLESS* rocks!"

~Jeanna Gabellini, author of *10 Minute Money-Makers* | www.MasterPeaceCoaching.com

"This is a powerful, life-shifting read for all those who dream about a different life, but can't seem to make it happen. This book is not about wishing on a star for a dream to materialize, it's about blasting through the mental barriers that keep you from success, and Thompson offers you an inspiring, easy-to-follow blueprint on how to do it. She truly understands the challenges and needs of her readers and offers both insightful wisdom and practical examples to guide you through the entire way. *fearLESS* is a must read; it's a real and relatable guide that will empower you to overcome the fears that stop you from realizing your dreams."

~Kimberly Morand, contributing author, *The Good Mother Myth: Redefining Motherhood to Fit Reality* and *Clash of the Couples*

"This book is liberating, inspiring, and thought-provoking. Nathalie Thompson knows her stuff and you will, too, by the end of this journey with her. Full of life-changing truths that will clear your path to "happily ever after", the concepts shared in *fearLESS* have the potential to make all the difference in how you engage life."

~Jeannette Maw, Good Vibe Coach | www.GoodVibeBlog.com

"If you've been struggling to create the kind of success you dream of in life, *fearLESS* is the blueprint that you've been waiting for. With gentle wit and soul-deep wisdom, Nathalie Thompson shares her experiences in a uniquely practical way, enabling her readers to effectively dismantle the fears that prevent them from realizing their own potential. You will appreciate her expert guidance as much as I did!

~René Trim, Chair, Ottawa Valley Crafts and Collectibles Guild | www.ovccshow.com

FEAR*LESS*

How to Conquer Your Fear, Stop Playing Small, and Start Living an Extraordinary Life You Love

Nathalie Thompson

Copyright © 2015 by Nathalie Thompson. All rights reserved.

No part of this publication may be reproduced, stored in a retrieval system, or transmitted in any form or by any means – electronic, mechanical, photocopying, recording, scanning, or otherwise – except for brief quotations in critical reviews or articles, without the prior written permission of the author.

The author of this book does not dispense medical advice or prescribe the use of any technique as a form of treatment for physical, emotional, or medical problems without the advice of a licensed physician, either directly or indirectly. Any use of information in this book is at the reader's discretion and risk. The advice and strategies contained herein may not be suitable for your particular situation, and you should always consult with a professional where appropriate. Neither the author nor the publisher shall be liable for any loss, claim, or damage resulting from the use or misuse of the suggestions made.

All trademarks and registered trademarks appearing in this book are the property of their respective owners.

For information visit www.VibeShifting.com.

Cover photo: © Jill Wellington, used with permission.
Cover design by Nathalie Thompson.

ISBN 978-0-9948844-0-4 (pbk)
ISBN 978-0-9948844-1-1 (ebk)

First Edition: January 2016

10 9 8 7 6 5 4 3 2 1

Dedicated to my greatest hero; it is said that there are some
who bring a light so great into the world
that even after they have gone the light remains.
You were one of those.

Forever in my heart, Daddy...

A LIFE LIVED IN FEAR IS A LIFE HALF-LIVED.
~FROM THE MOVIE "STRICTLY BALLROOM"

Contents

Introduction	1
Just Another Good Girl	2
Creating a Life of No Regrets	4
Making a Choice	5
From Dreamers to Doers	6
Chapter 1: Everyone Has Fears	9
What Could You Do…*If*?	10
The Path to Success	10
Why You Picked Up This Book	13
What This Book Will Do For You	15
The Guardian at the Gate	21
Building Your Dreams	24
Chapter 2: The Only Thing That's Stopping You	27
The "Safe" Route Isn't Guaranteed	28
Are You Sabotaging Yourself?	30
How to Deal With Self-Sabotage	33

Fear Is Not Real	35
The Best Thing That Could Happen	36
Go Big or Go Home	38
Crazy Enough to Change the World	40
Chapter 3: Can You Really Conquer Fear?	**43**
Inconsequential vs Important Fear	44
Mindset Matters	46
Attitudes Are Contagious	47
Expect Great Things	50
Dreams Are Not Enough	51
The Myth of the Overnight Success	53
Inspired Action vs Forced Action	55
Chapter 4: Your Fears, Unmasked	**59**
All Obstacles Can Be Overcome	60
The Biology of Fear	60
Negativity Spirals	61
How to Stop the Spirals	66
The Genie in the Bottle	69
Primary vs Secondary Fears	72
The Four Most Common Dream-Killing Fears	76
Chapter 5: The Fear of Failure	**79**
Famous "Failures"	80
Failure is Part of the Process	82

Perfectionism is a Bad Habit	83
How to Let Go of Perfectionism	85
Turning Your Doubts into Stepping Stones	87
Breaking the Worry Habit	91
If You Want to Get Good, You Must Get Started	93
The Real Key to Success	94
Chapter 6: The Fear of Success	**99**
Why Would Anyone Fear Success?	100
Do You Have a Fear of Success?	101
An Example of Fear of Success	104
How to Stop Procrastinating	107
Dream, Believe, Achieve	109
Making the Mental Shift	112
Chapter 7: The Fear of Judgement	**117**
Your Dreams Are Never "Wrong"	118
I'll Never Be Good Enough (Coping with Your Inner Critic)	121
Getting to Know Your Gremlins	121
How to Tame Your Gremlins	125
Sticks and Stones (Coping With Outside Critics)	127
What if The Critics Are Family?	132
Why Are Strangers More Supportive Than Family?	136
Strategies for Coping with Family Critics	138

Weathering the Storms	140
Chapter 8: The Fear of the Unknown	**143**
You Will Never Have All the Answers	144
The Greatest Risk	145
"But I Want to Be a Pirate!"	149
Creating Your Awesome List	151
Been There, Done That!	153
Dreams Don't Build Themselves	155
Mountain Climbing 101	158
Chapter 9: Strategies for FearLESSness	**163**
The Power of Why	164
Breaking Negative Thought Habits	168
Resistance is *Not* Futile	171
How to Identify Resistance	176
How to Eliminate Resistance	177
The Doorway to Your Dreams	179
Becoming Certain	180
Chapter 10: The Other Side of Fear	**185**
The Whisper Within	186
Why Be Different?	187
Making the Most of Opportunity	189
Gifts from the Universe	191
Becoming a Master of Synchronicity	192

Chapter 11: A Life Less Ordinary	197
A Commitment to Yourself	198
The Road Less Travelled	198
Your Next Chapter	200
Acknowledgements	203
Bonuses	205
Find Your FearLESSness	206
About the Author	207
References	208

Introduction

> IF YOU WANT SOMETHING YOU'VE NEVER HAD,
> YOU MUST BE WILLING TO DO SOMETHING YOU'VE NEVER DONE.
> ~Thomas Jefferson, 3RD President of the United States of America

It was just after two o'clock in the morning when my phone rang. I was instantly awake, knowing, in the very pit of my anxious stomach, who was calling and why. "We think you should come. Now." said the voice on the other end of the line, and I closed my eyes for a moment and prayed for the strength to get through the next few hours. I dressed as fast as I could while I waited for the friend with a car who had volunteered to drive me to my destination and I think we broke every speed limit in the city on the way across town, trying to make sure that I got there in time.

My father was heavily sedated. Everyone who had been with him that night had finally gone to bed, exhausted from coping with hours of his overwhelming agitation before the sedatives had kicked in and they had called me. And so it was that I was the only one awake in those early hours as I held his frail hand in the darkness, watching his breaths grow further and further apart until, eventually, they stopped altogether.

He had fought a two-and-a-half year battle with stage four metastatic colon cancer and had been told only two short weeks before that morning that it had become terminal and that he was being transferred to palliative care. Not one of us, least of all him, could wrap our heads around how quickly it had happened. Three weeks ago, they had told him he was going to start a new treatment protocol... and then an unexpected phone call (*a phone call!*) from his oncologist informed him that the latest scan results meant that there was nothing more to be done.

I had already lost my mother in a car accident when I was a child and my father had been my anchor point ever since. Losing him left me feeling adrift... and alone. I suppose, in hindsight, the experience spawned something of an existential crisis, in that it made me start questioning and re-evaluating everything. What did I want out of life? Why was I even here? What was the point of it all?

Just Another Good Girl

For as long as I can remember, I've been trying to make other people happy; a gifted student, I was the proverbial "good girl" who never got into trouble, and always conscientiously tried to be helpful when I could.

The first time I pulled straight-A's in grade school, I can still remember thinking how proud my father would be. In high school, I took all the courses he said were important (math and science) and dropped all the ones that I personally enjoyed (art, languages, and music). I applied to the "acceptable" programs in university, and ended up with degrees in both Cognitive Science and Education. I even got the "right" job in the computer field when I graduated. Eventually, I got married to a great guy, had two beautiful children, and ended up as a stay-at-home mother.

In other words, I did everything I was supposed to. I did everything right. And, to the outside observer, my life must have looked almost perfect. I should have been happy, but I wasn't. Something wasn't right, and hadn't been for a long time. A decades-long struggle with clinical depression had recently resurfaced in the form of a diagnosis of post-partum depression; my marriage had deteriorated to such an extent that when my husband and I actually bothered speaking to each other at all, it was mostly to snipe; I was constantly getting sick with every bug that went around; and I felt exhausted, drained, and despairing most of the time.

Identity Crisis

By the time my father became ill, I had started to realize what the problem was: I wasn't living the life I was meant to. I didn't regret the decisions I had made up until that point, and I wouldn't trade motherhood for the world. But I needed to be something more than "just" somebody's wife and somebody's mother. Don't get me wrong – these things are important, and they were important to me, too. But they based my identity on other people – *their* needs, *their* desires, and *their* dreams. And they didn't take into account my own dreams and the things that made me... *me*.

I felt as if I had spent my whole life giving up my own identity to become what other people needed and expected me to be. I didn't even know who I was anymore. With each passing year, I felt time flying by ever more quickly and I was afraid that I was never going to be able to do any of things that I had wanted to do with my life. I was afraid that one day time would run out, and I would never have done any of the things that I had always dreamed of doing. And that thought made me very, very sad.

Creating a Life of No Regrets

In her incredible book, *The Top Five Regrets of the Dying*, Bronnie Ware shared the experiences and insights she gained while working in palliative care. And she said that the most common regret expressed by the people she cared for during those years was that they wished they had had the courage to live a life that was true to themselves, rather than what was expected of them by other people. It's a thought that has been echoing through my mind ever since that dark, lonely morning on the other side of town.

My father's passing made me realize, once again, just how fleeting life on earth could be and I was determined that I was going to DO something with my life, with whatever time I had.

I did not want to get to the end of my days filled with regrets over all the things that I had wanted to do but had never had the guts to even attempt. I didn't want to spend my life trying to fit into the ideals of what everyone else (including my father) felt was a proper kind of life for me, at the expense of my own joy and happiness. And I didn't want to keep putting off things that were important to me for a "someday" that might never happen.

Teaching by Example

I also looked at my children, and wanted so much for them to be spared the kind of existence that so many people settle for.

I didn't want them to grow up to become what was expected of them; to be part of the majority of people who hate their jobs, counting down to retirement, and living only for the weekend. I wanted them to figure out what they were born to do and to *know* that they could go out there and do it, whatever it was.

And in order for them to learn this – in order for them to grow up with the kind of mindset and determination that would propel them forward into lives and adventures of their own choosing – I had to be the one to teach them, through my own example, that it was possible. And I was determined to figure out how to make that happen.

Come hell or high-water, I decided that I was going to make my dreams a reality, no matter what it took.

Making a Choice

The problem was that I didn't even know where to start. And the thought of moving forward towards any of those dreams of mine terrified me. Because I knew that things in my life were going to have to start changing – *I* was going to have to start changing – if I really wanted to make any of those dreams happen; if I really wanted to become the kind of person I knew, deep inside, that I was capable of being.

I knew at the time that the journey I was about to begin would require me to face some of my biggest fears head-on if I was ever going to achieve what I wanted to. The prospect was daunting — I have a lot of fears — but, having just watched one of the people I loved most in the entire world die, I was not prepared to settle for an average, auto-pilot, default life anymore.

So I opted for the extraordinary. I made a deliberate choice to figure out what it was that I really wanted in life and then go after it with everything I had in me, despite any fears that threatened to hold me back.

A Work in Process

It hasn't always been easy. There have been a lot of tears, and a lot of doubts going through this process. In some ways, it's been an extremely difficult few years. But at the same time, it's also been an amazing few years. In chasing down my dreams, I've learned an awful lot about myself. I've also met some incredible people in my quest, and I've done some of the bravest things that I have ever done.

I don't always know what I'm doing, and I don't always know what's going to happen next. I guess you could say that I'm still a work in process; I'm definitely not where I want to be yet, but I keep moving forward. And with every step that I take – with every fear that I face – I become stronger and my path becomes clearer.

From Dreamers to Doers

Let me show you how I did it. *fearLESS* is the distilled version of everything I've learned and put into practice along my journey. I've taken all the best strategies that I've used, all the insights that I've had, and all the experience that I've gained while working towards my own dreams and put it all together into a guide to make *your* journey easier.

This book isn't meant to be a fluffy pep talk for people who are happy to just fantasize about "someday"; this is a how-to manual for dreamers who want to become doers and turn those dreams into reality. This is your VIP access pass to the fast-lane, and it's going to get you through your biggest fears so that you can build your biggest dreams.

Are you ready?

Then let's get started...

Chapter 1: Everyone Has Fears

> WE FEAR THE THING WE WANT THE MOST.
> ~ROBERT ANTHONY, AMERICAN MOTIVATIONAL AUTHOR

What are you afraid of? I know there's something, because we're *all* afraid of something. I guarantee you that even the toughest MMA and UFC fighters out there have fears of their own, and even the most successful billionaire business tycoons and Hollywood A-Listers sometimes doubt themselves. Fear is just part of being human. It's how we handle our fears, however, that makes the difference between success and failure; it's how we choose to act on those fears that determines whether our dreams will wither or take flight.

If we allow fear to call the shots and dictate how we live our lives, that's when we allow failure to take over. But if we acknowledge the fear and choose to forge ahead with our dreams and goals anyway, success becomes almost inevitable. It may not happen in quite the way we had expected, but there is no way to really lose once we start facing our fear; we learn so much about ourselves and our capabilities in the process, that no matter what the outcome is, it can't be considered anything other than a success as long as we're prepared to try again and use what we've learned as building blocks for greater things.

What Could You Do...*IF*?

So often it happens that we put off doing what we most want to do in life because we're afraid that we're not good enough to pull it off; we're afraid that the road to success will be more than we can handle, or that we'll never be able to find that elusive path to begin with. And so our biggest dreams get pushed onto a shelf and left there to collect dust because of a false belief that we don't have what it takes to make those dreams happen.

The sad thing is that, for most of those dreams, if we just got started and kept plugging away at them they would, in fact, become a reality... *if*. If we weren't so paranoid about taking that first step when we couldn't see the entire path mapped out before us; if we weren't so scared of looking like an idiot if we messed up; if we weren't so convinced that everything had to be done exactly right out of the gate that we panicked over the thought of starting it at all.

The Path to Success

For some reason, we tend to assume that the people we see as successful knew what they were doing from the start and took a direct route to the top, stepping from one phenomenal success to another. We assume they always knew exactly what was going on at every moment, at every step of the journey. But I suspect that the reality is probably quite different. I suspect that most of those successful people we see out there had their own moments of doubt; their own moments of confusion; their own moments of panic and wondering "what the hell am I doing?"

In Chapter 5 you'll see that the real road to success looks less like a straight line and more like a circuitous path of ups and downs, and that the one thing that distinguishes those who succeed in making their dreams a reality from those who don't is tenacity: the determination to stick with it until it's done.

Success is a matter of trying different approaches to achieving your goals. If one approach doesn't work, then you analyze what went wrong and try again with a different tactic. You learn as much as you can from every failure so that your next attempt will work better. Eventually you figure it out and get to where you want to be.

But the secret is in making those attempts in the first place. You can choose the safe route and not try to build your dreams at all. And you'll live more or less the same kind of life that everyone else around you does. Or you can choose the alternate route, take some chances, and just maybe create everything that you've ever wanted for yourself.

KNOWING WHAT YOU'RE CAPABLE OF

In my earliest days of Toastmasters, a club member by the name of David Perry, an international executive recruiter and the author of *Guerrilla Marketing for Job Hunters 3.0* and *Hiring Greatness*, gave a toast for the evening and said: "May you always know what you are capable of before you need to."

No one at the meeting seemed to "get" it and I was bemused because, to me, this was a rather profound toast and, in my opinion, it was and is the key to everything. For those of us who have big dreams in our hearts, knowing what we are capable of before we need to is critically important because it will help us to get through the fear that springs up when we start taking real action towards those dreams and goals.

It's about believing in yourself and in your own ability to overcome any challenges that you may face; it's about understanding that if you really want something, there is always a way to make it happen; and it's about determination and ingenuity and not stopping until you've reached your goal, because anything else would be unthinkable.

YOU ARE STRONGER THAN YOU THINK

If there's one great truth that I've learned over the years, it's that you are *always* stronger than you think you are. This is especially true when it comes to your dreams and creating the kind of life you want to live. Once you've decided that you're ready to go for something, then no matter what the challenge is or how scary the situation may be, you are *always* strong enough to see it through, whether you know it yet or not.

The problem is that, sometimes, we let fear take root. And once we let that happen, obstacles suddenly become insurmountable and the fear we associate with venturing forth into unknown territory becomes sheer terror. And so we back off. We give in to the fear and we stay frozen in place where we are because we don't know which way to turn or what to do next.

And for some, it never goes beyond that. They stay where they are forever, and never find out what might have been. Their fears are strong enough to prevent them from even trying. And so they drop their dreams, leaving them behind for the security of the safer route.

Follow Your Heart, Follow Your Dreams

Imagine, however, what might happen if you let go of the fear; imagine if you could dare to face the fear and look beyond it. Imagine if you could turn that fear into an ally, and use it as a catalyst to do more and become more than you ever could have before.

And so, in true Toastmasters tradition, let me propose a toast to you today as you begin your own journey into understanding and overcoming your fears; as you begin the adventure of building the extraordinary: May you always believe in the importance of your dreams; may you always know that you have the power to make a difference in this world; and may you always know what you are capable of before you need to.

Fear is a normal reaction when facing the unknown. When you make that life-changing decision and commitment to follow your heart and follow your dreams, you're going to start heading in directions you've never gone before. And when this happens, fear is to be expected. But letting that fear dictate the terms of your life is an option, and you are free to choose otherwise. You are free to decide that your dreams are more important than your fears.

Why You Picked Up This Book

I'm guessing that you picked up this book because you have a big dream in your own life; something that means the world to you, but that you just haven't managed to make any real progress with yet. Maybe you've been holding that dream so close to your heart that no one else knows or even suspects that you have it. Maybe you've been feverishly pouring every spare minute you can find into making it happen, but you just can't bring yourself to let that dream out into the open where anyone else can see it. Or maybe you actually have revealed it to the world, but every time you start to make progress, something seems to stop you in your tracks or drop you all the way back to square one.

You know what the reason for all of that is, don't you? It's fear. Your own fears are keeping you from achieving your dreams and goals. In fact, those fears of yours are really the *only* thing that's holding you back from the success you're longing for.

THE REAL REASON YOU HAVEN'T "MADE IT" YET

Sure, it's easy to blame other people or circumstances for your lack of progress. It's easy to say that you'd be successful if only other people had "let you" be so. It's easy to say that you'd be out there accomplishing great things in your life if only you had more time, more money, more support, more connections, more education, or more whatever. But the truth is that all of these things are excuses; they are all just different masks for the *fear* that is the *real* reason at the heart of your lack of progress or achievement.

I'm not attacking you here, or even pointing fingers — because while this fear is the reason *you're* not making your dreams a reality, it's also the reason why I haven't made all of *mine* a reality yet, either. This fear is the reason why *all* of us hold ourselves back from achieving the kind of greatness that we are all capable of. And it's only when we are willing to take full responsibility for that - when we are willing to accept the fact that we are the ones who control our own lives and our own destinies - that we become able to do something about it.

WHAT ARE YOU AFRAID OF?

So tell me: What are you afraid of? What's holding you back from really going for it and crafting reality around that incredible vision in your mind? What is it that keeps you from your dreams?

- Are you afraid that you'll fail and be humiliated?
- Are you afraid that you'll succeed and that you won't be able to handle it when you do?
- Are you afraid of what others will think or say when they find out about your plans?
- Are you afraid of stepping forward into the unknown without knowing where the path will go?

You're not alone. These are the four most common dream-killing fears out there. These are powerful fears, and they are the ones that most often affect our ability to follow the inner guidance that lets us know what is truly the best path and direction for us. These are the fears that are most likely to prevent us from creating, and living, a life we truly love.

But this book is going to change all of that. In your hands is the guidebook for navigating the treacherous terrain of fear; this is the map that will help you to understand exactly how your fears are affecting you, and then get you through them so that they are no longer holding you back from what you want most in life: an extraordinary, happy, fulfilling existence, doing what you most want to do.

WHAT THIS BOOK WILL DO FOR YOU

Let me ask you this: If you knew that no one would say anything negative to you; if you knew that you could not fail; if you were absolutely fearless... what would you choose to do with your life? What would you do if you had no responsibilities, no financial worries, and no one to tell you what you "should" do? Yeah, yeah... you'd buy a car and dream home and maybe a private jet or an island or something, give some money to friends and family, and then lounge around on a beach for a couple of months, but what would you do *after* you got bored with all of that? What would you most *want* to do with your time if you didn't *have* to do anything?

Got the answer in your mind? Focus on it. I want you to think about every little detail of your life as if that dream were already a reality. Because by the time you're done with this book, you're going to be well on your way to being able to make it happen.

As you will learn in Chapter 2, the biggest obstacle standing between you and your dreams is your own mind, and this book is all about blasting through those mental barriers and getting you on track to where you want to be.

With this book, we're going to:

- determine which of the four most common fears are the biggest stumbling blocks between you and your biggest dreams;
- understand exactly how those fears work and how they're preventing you from accomplishing your goals and living your dreams; and
- implement specific, actionable strategies for coping with those fears and working through them.

By the time you've finished this book, you're going to know, without doubt, that you can achieve *anything* you set your mind to. You are going to recognize your biggest fears for the insubstantial shadows that they are, and you are going to know exactly how to work your way through them so that they no longer have the power to stop you from getting what you want in life. In short, we're going to turn you into a lean, mean, fear-busting, dream-building machine!

WHAT TO EXPECT WHEN USING THIS BOOK

When you start using the techniques and strategies in this book to work through your fears, you can expect to encounter resistance (you will learn more about that when we talk about strategies for fearLESSness in Chapter 9). For now, just know that resistance happens when you start trying to change ingrained, automated patterns of thought and behaviour; it's that reactive "push back" that you feel when you start thinking about and start moving towards a completely different way of doing things.

It can show up in subtle ways; in the seductive whisper of procrastination telling you that you don't really need to this *now*, for example. Or it can present itself more forcefully, like an invisible wall that slams into place before you with the instant thought that what you're considering is impossible.

When you decide that your dreams are more important to you than your fears and you make that deliberate choice to start dismantling your blocks and dissolving those fears, there *will* be fallout. You're trying to change some deeply ingrained habits that you have been running on automatic for years, maybe even decades, and trying to suddenly change that programming is going to cause some friction, not just within your own self, but also with those around you.

AS YOUR JOURNEY BEGINS

When you start moving through your fears, there are some common experiences that you can expect to go through.

In the early stages:
- Your inner critic will start to howl, and you're going to be terrified. You may feel overwhelmed with thoughts telling you that it can't be done; that you're a fool to even consider this; that nobody is ever successful doing what you want to do; that you're going to fall flat on your face and everyone will laugh and say "I told you so".
- The outside world will mirror these inner beliefs. Your closest friends and family members may echo these same sentiments back to you; they'll make it quite plain, either directly or indirectly, that they don't believe you can do this and that you're crazy to even try; they'll even try to make you feel like you're irresponsible or childish for continuing down this path.

When you're dealing with all of the rough patches, however, remember to keep yourself focused on what you're building because if you continue down your path and keep working to dissolve your fears and climb your mountains, you can then expect:

- A giddy feeling, a "rush" as you start to make progress and begin to realize that YOU CAN, and that this may actually be possible after all.
- Your self-confidence will start to increase and your fear will start to decrease as you successfully work through more and more of the obstacles that you once thought were insurmountable.
- Opportunities will start lining up as you keep moving forward and taking action to make your dreams a reality.

- The biggest external dream-bashers in your life may suddenly become your biggest supporters.

The key, of course, is keeping it together and getting through those first stages. I'm not going to lie to you and tell you that it will be easy, because it won't. When it feels like everyone around you is against you, and you're battling your own inner demons, and you're seeing little, if any evidence that what you're doing is actually working, keeping your mind clear enough to focus on and keep working towards that shining dream of yours is one of the hardest things that you will ever do.

DO YOU WANT TO EXIST OR DO YOU WANT TO LIVE?

The *easy* thing is to let the dream go. To give up in defeat, give in to your fears, and settle for the same kind life that everyone else around you has settled for themselves. It wouldn't be *all* that bad, after all... millions of people live that kind of existence every single day, and they seem to be getting by all right.

In the end, what it really comes down to is a choice between *existing* and *living*. You can choose to spend your life existing, or you can choose to go out there and *live* that life, to the greatest depth and breadth that you are capable of. But you are the only one who can decide if the possibility of living something extraordinary is worth the initial struggle. You are the only one who can decide if your dreams are worth the discomfort and growing pains of facing your fears and moving through them in order to get to the part where you are actually living those dreams.

. . . . .

How to Use This Book

In this book I have included a lot of theory and background because understanding what is actually happening inside of you when you are afraid of something will help you to work your way through those fears. But I have also made sure to include plenty of actionable strategies and exercises to help you blast through those blocks and start living your dreams.

This is meant to be more than just another book detailing the "why" of things; it's meant to be a practical "how-to" guide to effectively dealing with the internal issues that are keeping you from everything you want in life. To make things easier for you, at the end of each chapter of this book I have included:

- a summary of key points that I want you to remember;
- a checklist of the exercises detailed within the chapter, referencing the pages in which you can find those exercises again;
- links to downloadable bonus materials: worksheets, infographics, and templates to help you out with your exercises.

My suggestion is that you download the bonus material now and print out the worksheets so that you can do the exercises as you read through the book. You can get your bonus package here:

> http://www.VibeShifting.com/fearless-bonus.

What Do You Really Want?

Now that you know how to use the book, it's time to get down to business! Your first action strategy begins now: In order to begin overcoming your fears, it helps to take stock of where you're currently at. You need to get clear on what

Everyone Has Fears

it is that you really want in life, and then get equally clear on why it's important that you actually achieve it.

One of the most powerful motivators that you will ever have is your "why" (and we're going to talk more about that in Chapter 9). For the moment, though, all I want you to do is a simple two-part exercise, and the first part is this: write down your dream.

Take a moment to get clear about what, exactly, your dream is and put it down, on paper – no computer allowed. Why handwriting on paper? Because writing has been shown to use more areas of your brain than typing[1], and because writing activates an area of your brain called the Reticular Activating System (RAS)[2], which is a filtering system that decides what you pay attention to and how important the incoming information is.

The Guardian at the Gate

Your RAS acts as the guardian at the gate to your higher-level mind, or the executive assistant whose job is to prevent unimportant callers from taking up any of the boss's precious time.

Our brains, you see, are fed about 11 million bits of data every single second[3] — far too much for our conscious minds to cope with (current estimates say that we are only able to deal with between 16 and 50 bits of data per second[4]) — and it is our RAS that decides what's important enough, out of that torrent of data that is constantly streaming in, to be pushed up to conscious awareness.

Basically, most of the data coming into our brains is ignored; it is filtered out of our conscious reality in order to allow us to concentrate on what's actually important to our lives and our survival. Without this filtering system, the sensory overload resulting from that much data would leave us unable to function.

You can see examples of how this filtering system works and how data gets "upgraded" in importance in your own life. For example, when women are trying to conceive, or have recently had a miscarriage, they commonly report seeing pregnant women, or women with very young infants *everywhere*. And when people start shopping for cars, they often start seeing the same make and model that they are considering buying everywhere they go. This happens because your RAS has decided that these things are now important, so it starts paying more attention to them and bumping this data up from your subconscious mind and into your conscious awareness. The pregnant women and the car you're after were always there, but you never noticed them before because they weren't considered overly important.

Harnessing the Power of Your RAS

Writing your dream down on paper has the same RAS-activating effects as the examples above, and that system is now going to start paying more attention to all the little things around you that could help you turn that dream into reality. All those little details that you never even knew were there because your mind was filtering them out of your consciousness will get upgraded in importance and passed on to your conscious mind for higher-level processing.

In effect, you're programming your subconscious mind to start looking for ways to make your dreams a reality, and you're pressing the "go" button to set that program in motion. So get cracking; get yourself a nice notebook and your favourite pen, write down that dream of yours, and let's get this show on the road!

Costs and Benefits

The second part of this exercise is designed to get you really clear on what your fears are costing you. All you need to do is refer to the dream you wrote down in the first part of the exercise and then make a list of pros and cons; what are the benefits of making your dream a reality, and what are the costs of not doing so?

Write down what it would mean to you, and everything that could happen if you were to push through your fears and make your dream happen:

- What will achieving this goal allow you to do, have, experience, or become?
- What will achieving this goal allow the people you love most to do, have, experience, or become?

Then flip it around and think about everything that will happen if you *don't* do it. I want you to really understand what's at stake here, and what you're actually choosing between when you decide to either deal with your fears or to let them call the shots. So ask yourself what your life, and the lives of the people who are really important to you, will look like one way or the other in two years, five years, and ten years down the road, and write it all out.

It's a sobering comparison, isn't it? It's also completely your choice. If you're OK with a fear-based outcome to your life, then that's OK, and you certainly won't be the first person in history to have a book end up as a coaster.

If, however, you decide that your dreams are more important than your fears and that *this* is point in your personal timeline that spells the start of a brand-new story, then this book will help you get through those fears. This is the point where you start to build something extraordinary, something that may very well bring you everything you have ever wanted.

Building Your Dreams

Life is not a dress rehearsal. If you don't believe in reincarnation, this is the only life you will ever get to live and this is all the time you get in which to do everything you've ever wanted to do. And if you do believe in reincarnation, then this is only time you will ever experience *this particular* incarnation.

Either way, this experience of life that you are having right now is completely unique. So don't waste it. Go out there and be awesome; create your own road to success and start building your dreams! It's not going to be easy. But it is going to be worth it.

Chapter 1 Recap

❖ **Key Points to Remember:**

- All of us, from the greenest beginners to the most super-successful business tycoons and Hollywood A-Listers, are afraid of something; everyone has doubts and fears.
- The difference between an ordinary life and an extraordinary one is made when you decide whether you're going to let your fears call the shots in your life or not.
- If you want to succeed in creating your biggest dreams, you need to start believing in yourself and your own ability to overcome your fears.
- You can harness the power of your Reticular Activating System to help build your dreams.

❖ **Your Action Items:**

1. Get yourself a dream-building journal in which you can handwrite the exercises that you will find in this book. Or just download and use the bonus workbook and templates package that I've already created for you at:
2. http://www.VibeShifting.com/fearless-bonus
3. In your journal (or on the exercise page from the bonus pack), write down your dream.
4. Create a list of pros and cons: write down what you would gain by successfully building your dream, and what it would cost you if you failed to build it.

❖ **Download:**

- http://www.VibeShifting.com/fearless-bonus

Chapter 2: The Only Thing That's Stopping You

> I WRAPPED MY FEAR AROUND ME LIKE A BLANKET;
> I SAILED MY SHIP OF SAFETY 'TIL I SANK IT.
> ~The Indigo Girls, American Folk-Rock Musicians, "Closer to Fine"

I keep a sticky-note at the top of my computer screen, and it says "you can have results or you can have excuses". It's my reminder that the only one who can make things happen in my life is me, so I'd better get moving and get things done, no matter how scared I am about pushing myself out of my nice, safe, comfort zone.

Sometimes we use fear as a safety net, allowing it to give us an acceptable reason for not taking the risk of going out and living the kind of life we most want for ourselves. We wrap ourselves in this cocoon because it feels safer to let the fear control us than it does to face it and take that first trembling step forward, toward the goals we so desperately want to achieve.

But here's the thing: that safe little cocoon we think we have is just an illusion. We may think we're taking the responsible, guaranteed route that seems to be the one approved by everyone around us. But there are no guarantees in life. And the longer we hide ourselves away in those cocoons, the more likely we are to end up smothering ourselves in them.

What this all boils down to, of course, is that the only thing that can stop you from achieving your goals and turning your dreams into reality is YOU; *your* thoughts, *your* beliefs, *your* expectations, *your* choices, and *your* actions. Your dreams depend on you and you alone.

THE "SAFE" ROUTE ISN'T GUARANTEED

In his May 2014 commencement address[5] to the graduating class at the Maharishi University of Management, actor Jim Carrey talked about how his father had great comedic talent but that he had never believed that a career in comedy was possible, so he chose the safe route and became an accountant, believing that this was the wiser choice for stability and security. But years later, he was laid off from that "safe" job. Carrey said that this taught him that "you can fail at what you don't want, so you might as well take a chance on doing what you love."

He went on to say that too many people choose their path out fear, disguised as practicality. It's something that made a lot of sense to me, and something I've thought a lot about since first listening to his speech. Why do we make big decisions in life based on fear rather than on what our deepest, inner wisdom is so urgently whispering to us? When it comes to our direction in life, we put more stock in the opinions of just about everyone around us *except* the one person who has the most at stake: our own self.

YOU'RE THE ONLY ONE WHO KNOWS WHAT'S BEST FOR YOU

We spend so much time asking other people for advice about every aspect of our lives, but the problem with handing our power over to other people in this way is that it never works. You know from experience exactly what happens when you start with the never-ending polling of other people's opinions: they're oh-so-willing to give them to you, but instead of jumping up and shouting "Eureka! That's it!" and rushing off to joyfully implement their brilliant advice, you usually end up responding with a half-hearted "maybe you're right..." And even if you do end up acting on their advice, there's no joy in it.

You know why that is, don't you? When you start polling for other people's opinions like that, you're not really looking for advice because deep inside, *you already know what you want.* You *know* what you want to do. You *know* which direction you want to go in. And you *know* what it is that you are meant to do. But you're desperately looking for someone else to back you up on all of that; you want someone else to tell you that you're doing the right thing and that you're not crazy. You're looking for someone else to assuage your fears.

But no one else can tell you what the best path for you is. YOU are the only one who knows what's best for you. And the surest route to lifelong misery is to ignore that inner knowing; to give into your fears of what *could* happen if you step outside of the mainstream, and to spend your days trying to fit into somebody else's idea of who you should be. Spend enough time listening to everyone else's confused and often contradictory ideas about what's best for you, and you'll end up going nowhere and doing nothing that ever matters to you.

Are You Sabotaging Yourself?

The big question, of course, is: If you already know what's best for you and what you want to do in life, then why the heck aren't you doing it already? It's called *self-sabotage*, and it's one of the most common consequences of the unresolved subconscious fears that most of us have surrounding our biggest dreams and goals.

The most obvious example of self-sabotage at work is the situation that most of us have experienced at one point or another where something we've been working on seems to be going really well, progress is actually being made, and then all of a sudden the self-doubt bursts in out of nowhere. So we immediately get cold feet and start to back-peddle, quickly unravelling all the painstaking progress we've made up until that point.

But where does it come from? What causes us to sabotage our own dreams like that? For so many people, by the time we've reached adulthood, we've spent so long trying to meet the expectations of other people and society as a whole; we've spent so much time trying to fit ourselves into a mould that we were never meant to fit into that we've lost sight, on that conscious level, of what it is that we've always *known* we were meant for.

Nice Girls Don't

This happens with everyone to one extent or another, but it's a particularly common phenomenon with women. As women, we've been taught since childhood, whether directly or indirectly, that nice girls take care of other people. Despite all the advances that have been made with women's rights over the years, we've still got this ingrained belief that we're supposed to put our own needs aside because they're not as important as looking after other people's needs and making sure that everyone else around us is happy.

So we learn to tune out all those "whispers from within" – we learn to stop listening to that little voice inside of us that tells us what we're here for and what we're meant to do, because we've been taught that it's selfish to concentrate on ourselves. We put all our own dreams, ambitions and needs aside and we focus ourselves on being useful to other people; on making sure our husbands and our kids and all the other people in our lives are looked after, even if it means that we're not looking after ourselves.

But that kind situation is unstable. You can't keep pushing aside your own needs and stifling your own dreams without consequence. Something has to give, and there's always some kind of a backlash. And I think this is one of the reasons why there is such a high rate of depression among women. When you lose touch with that centre – that sense of who you really are – it has a very detrimental effect on both your mental and physical health.

Not only that, but the longer this goes on, the more you lose touch with that inner guidance; if you've taught yourself to stop listening to those whispers, it can become incredibly difficult to hear them again. And that's often where that sense of being lost and unable to decide what you want to do comes from. You know you're meant to do *something*, but you can't find your direction or your compass point anymore.

Scary Inner Critics

Now, how does this cause you to sabotage yourself? Because you've spent so long trying to be everything for everyone else, and because you've had a lifetime of false learning that says no one is going to love you unless you're sacrificing yourself for someone else, whenever you start moving in a particular direction that's important to you, all the scary, negative voices of your inner critics start coming out of the woodwork and undermining your efforts to create any kind of success for yourself.

You start moving in a particular direction, and maybe start making some real progress, and all of a sudden you start having these horrible thoughts:

- "Who am I kidding? I don't have what it takes to pull this off. This will never work!"
- "What if people don't like me anymore if I do this?"
- "My husband thinks this is a waste of time. Maybe he's right."
- "What about the kids? If I start getting busy with this, what will it do to them?"
- "Maybe this isn't what I really want anyway."

All these negative thoughts and fears start swirling through your mind and undermining your efforts to create what you really want because you *can't* be successful. You're not *allowed* to be because *nice girls* aren't successful themselves; they're supposed to help *other* people become successful, instead. And so, once again, you're back to square one, and wondering what the hell you want to do with your life, and why you can never seem to make anything happen for yourself.

How to Deal With Self-Sabotage

So that's where this comes from. But what do you do about it? How can you reconnect with that inner wisdom and learn to start hearing that voice within you once again? How can you find your direction and keep yourself from succumbing to those nasty inner critics that tell you that you can't? There are a few steps that you can take to help you with this...

1. Take Some Much-Needed "Me" Time

Schedule some time when you won't be interrupted by family or any outside responsibilities – time to just be by yourself and unwind a little.

Finding time for silence and solitude, when you can just sit with your own thoughts and feelings, will allow you to start reconnecting with what your heart has always been trying to tell you, but you've just been too busy to hear. Try to remember what it is that you've always wanted to do, and ask yourself if this is still something that is important to you. Try to remember what your dream really is.

2. Figure Out What Scares You

The next thing to do is to ask yourself what it is that scares you most about the possibility of achieving this goal. If you had a magic wand that you could wave and instantly make yourself super-successful with this dream of yours, what would you be feeling?

Make a list: write each of your fears down, and be totally honest about them – even if your logical mind tells you it's a ridiculous fear, if it's something that comes up in this exercise, add it to your list.

3. ANALYSE YOUR FEARS

Now, for each of those fears, I want you to really think about it. How likely is it that the things you fear most would actually happen? For instance, would your kids really hate you if you suddenly had something in your life that made you really happy and excited? Wouldn't the fact that you're happier and more engaged in life just make their lives that much better?

For the fears that actually have some sort of realistic possibility, think about what you could do now to mitigate those fears; create a plan for how you could deal with them before they ever happen. If you have contingency plans in place for the things you fear, then that often goes a long way to alleviating those fears.

4. REMEMBER WHY YOU HAVE YOUR DREAMS IN THE FIRST PLACE

Finally, I want you to remind yourself that your dreams are important. Not just to you, but to the entire world. They are your little bit of magic – the gift that you came here to share. And the best thing that you can do for those you care about most is to become all that you are capable of becoming. When you allow yourself to shine, you encourage all those around you to do the same. And isn't that the best gift you could ever give to anyone?

You can do, have, or become *anything* that you want in life; there are no limitations to what you are capable of achieving, except for the ones you place on yourself. It doesn't matter where you started from or what your circumstances are; the only one with the power to make you succeed or fail in life is *you*.

Fear Is Not Real

In the movie *After Earth*, starring Will Smith as the ghost ranger, Cypher Raige, there is a point where Smith's character says to his son: "Fear is not real. The only place that fear can exist is in our thoughts of the future." In essence, our fears are entirely imaginary; they are based entirely on things that we think *may* happen in the future – but those things don't exist right now and may never even become a reality.

So why do we attach such strong emotions and importance to them? Even if there is a tiger standing right in front of you, your fear is based on the thought that it *might* eat you, even if at the moment it is *not* eating you, and even if it may choose to ignore you, walk away, and *never* eat you. *Fear is not real.* Danger, as Smith's character goes on to say, is very real, but fear is entirely based on hypothetical scenarios about what *could* happen.

A Paradigm Shift

When I first saw the scene in *After Earth*, it was a paradigm-shifting moment for me. It made me realize just how ridiculous most of the fears that I had around my dreams really were, and it was one of the key moments in helping me get through them (thank you, Will Smith).

What I realized was that all our fussing and fretting over our imagined fears just makes us miserable in the present and attracts more stuff for us to worry about. The more importance we attach to something, the more we seem to worry about it and the bigger our fears seem to get, until we've got ourselves in full-fledged panic mode, imagining all the worse possible outcomes to the situation and freaking ourselves out over how we will ever possibly be able to deal with it.

But in reality, most of those fears that we've dredged up out of the darkest little corners of our minds will never, ever come to pass. They are doomsday scenarios that really aren't, and never were, in the realm of possibility. We get ourselves stressed out and panicked for no good reason whatsoever, all because of our dysfunctional habit of imagining the worst thing that could happen.

THE BEST THING THAT COULD HAPPEN

But what if we turned all of that on its head? What if, instead of imagining the worst possible outcome to a situation, we let ourselves imagine the *best* thing that could happen? Think of the energy shift that would bring! Think of the sense of relief, the stress reduction that would happen if we focused on the potential for positive outcomes instead of the negatives.

Think of what you could build with the energy and excitement of those kinds of thoughts. What could you do if you were focused on all the things that could go *right* with respect to your big dream, for instance? What great things could you build if you were concentrating on the *best* thing that could happen if you went for it, rather than fearing the worst that could happen?

PERMISSION TO BE HAPPY

Give this experiment a try: Pick one thing about your dream that really scares you. Then take the next five minutes and give yourself permission to vividly imagine everything turning out in the perfect way. Go full-out, pie-in-the-sky, rose-coloured-glasses, Pollyanna's-Got-Nothing-

On-Me perfection; for the next five minutes, imagine every single detail of that scenario working out in the best, most advantageous, happiest way possible!

It's only for five minutes, so why are you hesitating?

Is it because you really don't think it's possible for things to turn out that way? Is it because you don't want to be disappointed? Is it because you think someone else would think you're a fool for being so blindly optimistic? Is it because, deep down, you don't really believe that you deserve to have things turn out that well?

These feelings are telling you something about your internal, subconscious beliefs. They're telling you what you really expect from life. And if the thought of being sublimely happy and positive for as short a period as five minutes is making you uncomfortable, then maybe it's time to start re-evaluating what you think life is really all about.

In the meantime, I'd like you to try the above exercise again. Really try it. Get a kitchen timer and set it for five minutes (and if you really can't handle that much awesome all at once, then start with two minutes) and let yourself imagine your life the way you most want it to be.

Alternatively, you can try writing out your ideal scenario and putting it all down on paper. Either way, you are hereby given permission to be happy for five whole minutes. You can go back to your worries and your fears after the timer goes off, if you really feel the need to. But for this time, let all of the worry and the stress go and just *imagine*.

In Chapter 9 you're going to learn that it is the energy, the feelings, and the *expectations* that you have about your circumstances that create your experiences. When you start to shift those expectations, you start to shift your reality. If you can dream and believe it, you can *always* achieve it. So what's the best thing that could happen?

Go Big or Go Home

Here's an interesting thought: what if your dreams are *supposed* to scare you? What if it's that surge of adrenalin-induced energy that is meant to be a sign to you that you're on the right path? Nobel Peace Prize winner and 24th President of Liberia, Ellen Johnson Sirleaf once said that "If your dreams don't scare you, they are not big enough." So, what if it's that tingle of fear that indicates that *this* is THE DREAM for you, the one that you're truly meant to dedicate yourself to and bring forth into reality?

When I was in university working on my first degree, my roommate was a highly competitive die-hard sports fan who used to say "go big or go home" whenever we'd go out to toss the Frisbee™ around or play any kind of game. She meant that if you're not going to bring your "A-game" and give it your best, then don't bother playing at all. I thought it was a good phrase and it's stuck with me ever since because I firmly believe that each and every one of us has the power to change the world and make it better – but we can't do that by playing it safe and avoiding everything that scares us. If we want to make a difference in life, then we have to step up to the plate and *own* those dreams of ours. We have to be willing to go big, or we really might as well go home.

Stop Playing Small

Nelson Mandela once said that "There is no passion to be found playing small – in settling for a life that is less than the one you are capable of living." It's a sentiment that was also echoed by Dr. Abraham Maslow, one of the founders of the field of humanistic psychology, who said that "If you plan on being anything less than you are capable of being, you will probably be unhappy all the days of your life."

Back in April of 2014, I took a trip to another city to go to a concert with my sister. It was a Nana Mouskouri concert (yes, I have *very* eclectic tastes in music), and this was her final tour; she was eighty years old. As I was listening to her, I was struck by how much she obviously loved what she did. You could see it; you could feel it. This woman *loved* to sing and she loved to perform. And I was so inspired.

And that was when I heard the voice within me, and it wasn't even a whisper – it was a demand, a thunderous commandment, and it said "STOP PLAYING SMALL!" Over and over again I heard it: "*Stop playing small! Stop playing small!*"

I knew what it meant. The voice was saying: Stop holding yourself back. Stop being afraid. Stop worrying about outside opinion. Stop obsessing about the endless "what if" scenarios and just take the chance to become all that you *know* you are capable of. Be brave. Do the scary things, because they are what will bring you to where you want to be.

All the way home on the train I thought about it. How, exactly, does one just suddenly stop playing small? How do you make that shift when you've spent your whole life "being the good girl you've always had to be"[6] and doing whatever was expected of you? And I think that the most important step is actually just to make the decision – to decide, once and for all, that it's time to change, time to do whatever it takes to make the dream a reality. No more excuses. No more delays.

Make the decision, wholeheartedly and without reservation, commit utterly to becoming, and then trust that the right actions will become apparent at the right time. Trust. Have faith. Believe. And then jump... no matter how scared you are.

Shining Your Light

At some point, you have to let go of the fear. Or at least, you have to look it in the eye and then do your thing anyway. Because at some point you realize that even if everything goes to hell, at least you gave it your best shot, and now you know. And that is better than always wondering what would have happened... *if*. It's better than watching time slip away and living with endless regret because you never even took that chance to really go for it and let yourself shine.

And what's more, I'm convinced that the only way to really make a difference in this world is to go all out at what calls to you most strongly. Whatever it is - accounting or acting, painting or politics, calculus or crochet - whatever it is that makes you feel most alive is what you *should* be doing. You can make a difference in this world by doing what you do, and by doing it to the very best of your abilities. And you can't do that by playing small. You can't do that by holding back. You cannot do that by dimming your light.

Crazy Enough to Change the World

When I first started VibeShifting.com, I didn't tell anyone I knew anything about it. I was too afraid that people would laugh or make fun of me for starting such a "woo-woo" blog focused on mindset, success, and turning dreams into reality. But the key point is that I did, in fact, start it. And by consistently keeping at it, despite my fears, that little blog grew into an internet presence that now helps thousands of people all around the world to change their lives for the better.

If you want to be the change, then you have got to take the risk of putting yourself out there. You have to be willing to put some substance behind your ideas and your dreams, to put them out there before the crowd and to be strong enough to keep working at it even if people laugh or say mean things. Because most of the people who will try to bring you down had dreams of their own that they gave up on, and seeing anyone else make progress towards theirs just reminds them of what they threw away. You have to remember what Steve Jobs, founder of Apple Inc. said - that "it's the people who are crazy enough to think they can change the world who actually end up doing it".

DREAM BIG, DREAM BOLD

Regret is a painful thing. So dream as big and as bold as you can, and don't be afraid to go out and make those dreams happen. Don't hold anything back because the most important gift you can give to this world and to the people you care most about is to become all that you are capable of becoming and to shine as brightly as you can. By doing so, you will inspire everyone around you to do the same, and just imagine what a world it could be if we all did that.

Chapter 2 Recap

- ❖ **KEY POINTS TO REMEMBER:**
    - The standard "safe" route isn't guaranteed, and no one has a better idea of what's best for you than YOU.
    - The habit of self-sabotage usually comes from a learned belief that it is wrong to be successful.
    - Fear is entirely imaginary. What you are afraid of is a hypothetical construct about what you think *could* happen in the future, even though it *hasn't* happened and *may never* happen.
    - You will never achieve what you most want to in life if you keep holding yourself back, so stop playing small and start doing the scary things!

- ❖ **YOUR ACTION ITEMS:**
    1. Do the exercises for dealing with self-sabotage on page 33.
    2. Take 5 minutes to imagine the best possible outcome to something that really scares you about moving forward with your dream.
    3. Think about ways in which you've been holding yourself back and playing small up until now. Make a list and pick one item that you will commit yourself to moving forward on this week!

- ❖ **DOWNLOAD:**
    - http://www.VibeShifting.com/fearless-bonus

Chapter 3: Can You Really Conquer Fear?

> Courage is not the absence of fear,
> but rather the judgment that something else
> is more important than one's fear.
> ~Ambrose Redmoon, American Writer

There are two key aspects to being able to work your way through your fears, and these keys are: *mindset* and *action*.

When we talk about conquering your fears, what we're really talking about is learning to ease your fears so that they no longer act as a paralytic that keeps you from doing the all-important action steps that are necessary for turning your dream into reality. And that requires a two-pronged approach of working with your *thoughts and beliefs* about what is actually possible in your life, and with your *willingness and ability* to actually follow through and DO what is necessary to achieve your milestones and goals.

Will you ever be truly fearless? I hate to break it to you, but no, that will never happen. You will never get rid of all of your fears because fear is part and parcel of the human experience. More than this, you would never want to completely do away with fear because it's there for a reason.

There *are* good aspects to fear: it makes you aware of potential danger, it galvanizes you to take preventative action in the face of possible threats, and it keeps you from getting complacent and losing your edge. Fear has its uses. It's only when you allow your fears to dictate the course of your life that it becomes a problem.

You will never be completely fearless, but you *can* learn to fear *less*. And you can condition yourself to keep moving toward your dreams despite whatever fear remains.

Inconsequential vs Important Fear

In terms of moving through your fears, it's important to note that not all of your fears need to be conquered. Wasting your time and energy on inconsequential fears will just distract you from the real work of getting through the important ones. Differentiating between these two kinds of fear, however, is sometimes confusing. How do you know when fear is irrelevant versus when it's holding you back? How can you actually tell when fear is an issue?

The way to tell the difference is to ask yourself if the fear is preventing you from doing something that's important to you. If the fear is keeping you from doing something you don't care about, it's not an issue, but if you know that you would regret *not* doing something, yet fear is keeping you from doing it, then there's a problem.

Fears that Don't Matter

For example, I don't do spiders. I *really* don't do spiders. I'm terrified of them. You will never, *ever* see me holding a tarantula in my hand, and I will never allow one to set even one creepy-crawly foot across the threshold of my doorway, no matter how "cool" my son happens to think they are. Not ever. Can I ever foresee a time when I will regret not holding an enormous, hairy, horrible spider in my hand, or regret not letting my child have one as a pet? Definitely not.

Likewise, is there anywhere in the world that I want to visit where there is high likelihood of me having to cope with gigantic spiders? Not really. Is there any other circumstance in my life in which my fear of spiders could cause me any form of regret? Not that I can think of. Therefore, fear of spiders is not really an issue for me.

Fears that Matter

On the other hand, another fear that I have is a fear of heights. You will never, *ever* see me bungee jumping, riding rollercoasters, downhill skiing, or setting foot on a balcony above the fourth floor, for example. Are any of these experiences things that are important to me? Do I care about any of these things? Do I have a burning desire to experience any of them in my life? Nope. So, on those points, my fear of heights is not an issue.

But I *do* want to see England someday. I want the experience of going to London and seeing the city, and of going to Stonehenge and the Cotswolds and all those other places in the pictures from England that fire up my imagination and make that whole concept of "going to England" so exciting for me. If I never go to England in my life it *will* be something that I regret. Therefore, if my fear of heights were enough to keep me from getting on an airplane and flying across an ocean at 30 000 feet in order to get to England *then* it would definitely be an issue.

THE LITMUS TEST

So here's the litmus test: pick one of the dreams or goals that you have for yourself, but which you haven't achieved or experienced yet. Now ask yourself this: "If I die tomorrow, will I regret not having done this?" I don't generally advocate such morbid thinking, but in this case it's actually helpful. Realizing that there will, one day, be an end to one's life does tend to have a very focusing effect on people. So use it. Figure out what's really important to you; if the thought of dying without having achieved or experienced something on your "bucket list" really bothers you, then you know that the fear surrounding that experience or achievement is something you *need* to deal with.

You can find ways to face those fears, work through them, and still do whatever it is that you most want to do in life. And that process begins inside your own head; it begins with your mindset and the way you think about your dreams, your abilities, and the possibility of you ever being able to do the things you most want to.

MINDSET MATTERS

Something that I emphasize on my blog and with the people I coach is that *everything* has to do with mindset. Your entire experience of life, everything that you will ever do, have, or accomplish depends on what's going on inside your own head. So if you want to see a different story outside of you, then you have to start with the things you're telling yourself on the inside. As within so without; it's all an inside job.

What you frequently think about affects your beliefs, which affects your expectations, which affects your *actions*. If you don't believe that what you want in life is possible for you, then you won't even bother trying. Likewise, if you don't believe you *deserve* what you want, then you'll always be undermining your own efforts to achieve it. How you *think* and *feel* about what you're trying to achieve has an enormous impact on your ability to actually make it happen.

Expectations Are Key

When it comes to manifesting the kind of life experience that you most want for yourself, your expectations are key. When you dread something (like not having enough money, for example), think about the kind of energy that puts out into the Universe; think about what that dread tells you about what you *expect*, in terms of financial abundance in your life.

As another example, when you're jaded about relationships and fall into the fearful trap of thinking that "all guys are like that" or "women always do that", think about the energy you're sending out into the world and what that jadedness says about your expectations regarding the possibility of ever having a loving, fulfilling relationship.

If you believe that money is hard to get, or that you will never find the right person, your subconsciously controlled actions will ensure that this, in fact, becomes your reality.

Attitudes Are Contagious

Something to keep in mind when you start thinking about your mindset and thought patterns is that the connections you have with other people have a real impact on your life because the people you surround yourself with and spend the most time with affect your mood, your perspective and your attitude.

Attitudes are contagious, and if you're constantly bombarded by negativity via other people's comments and actions, it *will* start to rub off on you. And when you have a big dream that you want to turn into reality – when you're trying to do something extraordinary with your life – this negative cesspool swirling around you can spell the end of that dream before it even gets out of the gate.

For example, how likely are you to be able to achieve your dream if those around you are constantly telling you it can't be done, that dreams are foolish and futile, that life's a bitch and then you die, that the 1% has screwed over the little guy, that people are stupid and mean and selfish and evil and that's just the way it is. If you're like me, you can feel the downshift in your energy and mood just by reading all that negative muck.

But now, I want you to think about the fact that dreams come true for people every single day; that every great achievement in this world started out as *somebody's* dream; that the Universe itself is waiting with bated breath to see what you're going to do with *your* dream; that most people are wonderful, helpful and good; that there is kindness and love and laughter and joy all around us; and that anyone who wants to can do and become whatever he or she wants. Can you feel the difference? Can you *feel* the upshift when you read those words?

THE "FLAVOUR" OF YOUR THOUGHTS

This is why it's so important to be careful with who and what you're surrounding yourself with in your everyday life. This, incidentally, is also why so many of us who work in this field have stopped watching the evening news. The media has a saying that "if it bleeds it leads" – the whole industry has admitted that it is skewed to showcase the bad stuff in the world and to focus on the worst possible elements of human nature. And if you are constantly subjecting yourself to that, it can't help but have an effect on how you *perceive* the world. If all you hear day in and day out is how much everything sucks, of *course* you're going to start feeling the same way.

What I'm saying here is that your life will take on the characteristics, or *flavour*, of your thoughts, and your thoughts are affected by the company you keep and the attitudes you surround yourself with. So if you're trying to make some real, positive changes in your life, you may need to start re-evaluating the wisdom of some of those connections.

Evaluating Your Connections

How do you feel when you listen to your music? What do you feel like doing after you watch some of your usual TV shows? What do you think of the world after you read the news? If all any of this does for you is make you depressed, angry, exhausted or afraid, then maybe it's time to flip the channel or upgrade your connections by picking better messages to expose yourself to.

Likewise, do the people you spend the most time with highlight your best qualities or do they constantly point out your worst qualities? Are their conversations focused on fear or on hope? Do they inspire you to keep going and achieve the things you want to, or do they constantly tell you all the reasons why they think your dreams are ridiculous, selfish, unacceptable or otherwise unattainable? Do you feel more upbeat when you're around them or do you feel drained? If your connections with others are detrimental to you, if they're making you feel more bad than good, then maybe it's time to let go. Let go, and trust that the *right* connections are out there waiting for you.

EXPECT GREAT THINGS

Former NBA basketball star Michael Jordon once said that "you must expect great things of yourself before you can do them". And this is so true; the most life-transforming thing you will ever realize is just how powerful you really are. You really *can* do anything you set your mind to.

The hardest part about coming to that realization and unleashing your power is the lifetime of conditioning you've had that has taught you to think otherwise. You've been brainwashed, my friend. And it's time you shook off that old programming and started calling the shots for yourself. If you want to create great things in your life, then you have to start by *expecting* yourself to achieve great things.

IT STARTS WITHIN

If you choose to surround yourself with negativity and fear, those attitudes will soak their way into your subconscious and colour everything that you think, say and do. But if you surround yourself with positivity, optimism, encouragement and hope, then *these* are the things you will start to create. You experience what you expect to experience in life. So if you continue to focus on your fears, and all the reasons why you think you *can't* do something, then you won't do it. It's as simple as that.

You must change the way you look at things if you want to see the circumstances of your life start to change. It has to start within, and it has to start with you. YOU are the most powerful creative force in your life. Not your boss. Not your spouse. Not your annoying neighbour. Not the guy who got the promotion instead of you. It's YOU. You control your own experience. And this includes whether or not you are successful in building your own dreams.

Choose to hold yourself to higher standards; choose to believe that anything you want to do, have, or become in life is possible for you; and choose to let go of any negative, unproductive, fearful attitudes that are holding you back from building that dream.

DREAMS ARE NOT ENOUGH

The second key to working your way through fear is *action*. What you absolutely must remember about dreams, fear, and creating a life you love is that *dreams are not enough*.

Most of the people who buy self-help books never implement what they learned in those books – they don't actually DO any of the suggested exercises or follow any of the strategies they are given in those books. And the problem with this is that knowledge means nothing until you use it. You can read every book you want to that relates to your dream or goal, you can learn everything there is to know about fear and what to do about it, but until you actually use that knowledge, you're never actually going to get through your fears or create anything new.

Likewise, you can sit around singing "Kumbaya" and watching motivational clips on YouTube for as long as you want, and yes, you'll feel great about your dream – for a short time. But that wonderful dream that feels so awesome when you think about it is only ever going to be a fantasy unless you get out there and start building it. If that dream is ever going to go anywhere or mean anything, then you have to get it *out* of your head and *into* the real world. And to do that, you must take action and start *doing*, despite your fears.

INTEREST VS COMMITMENT

When it comes to your dream — that vision you have in your head of what you'd like your life to be like — you need to ask yourself if you're really committed to the dream, or if you're just interested in it, because there is a big difference between the two.

If you don't want it enough to go all out; if you're not willing to go the distance and put everything you've got into making it happen; if you're not prepared to take risks to see it through, then you're not committed to it, you're just interested in it. Interest is OK. It's good to be interested in things. But interest doesn't build dreams, and dabblers are not the architects of greatness. Only commitment can turn a dream into reality.

For example, a lot of people like the idea of running their own business and being their own boss, but only committed people are willing to go the distance, put in the hours, take the risks, accept full responsibility for success or failure, and be comfortable enough with the lack of security, stability (and pension and benefits packages) to make it happen. When people realize that an entrepreneur's ability to pay her bills, buy her groceries, and meet her mortgage payments is entirely her own responsibility, that entrepreneurial shine tends to wear off rather quickly for most people.

Most people like to daydream about things, but they're not willing to put in the kind of work and take the kind of risks that are necessary to actually build those dreams. The ones that are willing to do what it takes prove it with their actions. If you say that you want something, but your actions aren't backing that up, then you don't want it badly enough. You need to align your actions with what you say you want if you ever expect to have anything to show for it.

THE MYTH OF THE OVERNIGHT SUCCESS

Success does not happen overnight. It comes from years of dedication and willingness to do the work to actually build *in reality*, that vision that once existed only in your mind. You've got to be willing to walk the talk if you really want to live that dream.

The late American actor Leonard Nimoy became a science fiction legend because of his role as the half-Vulcan, Spock, in the classic *Star Trek* television series. His leap into fame may have appeared sudden to the outside observer, but he had been working as an actor, taking on more than 50 small roles and supplementing his income with multiple odd jobs, for about fifteen years before being cast in the "big break" role that launched him into global super-stardom.[7]

Likewise, American film director George Lucas is known worldwide as the creative force behind the entire *Star Wars* franchise. It's because of him that phrases such as "May the force be with you" and "Luke, I am your father" are permanently etched into the memories of most of the Western world. But the first *Star Wars* movie was not released until 1977 – almost two decades after Lucas had already started making movies.[8]

There is an awful lot that goes on behind the scenes of what we like to think of as "overnight success" stories; all the nitty-gritty, un-glamourous, stuff that we just never hear about. There is fear and there is failure; there are ups and there are downs; there is exhilaration and there is despair. There is a dedication and commitment to the dream, and a determination to solidify the insubstantial *vision* into something real by taking consistent, ongoing *action*.

YOU GET WHAT YOU PUT INTO IT

It's so easy to just sit there and wish for something better to come along. And we all have days where we're tired and we're discouraged and all we want is for someone to take us by the hand and tell us where to go or what to do next; we just want someone to make it easy for us. But there's no satisfaction in easy. And no one is coming to rescue you. You get what you put into life. And by making a choice to start taking action and *doing* something, you start to build up momentum, and inertia starts to work for you.

Newton's First Law of Motion tells us that an object at rest tends to stay at rest and an object in motion tends to stay in motion. This principle is as applicable to your life as it is to physical objects. As you start doing, you start getting inspired to do even more, and then even more. Ideas will start flowing, energy is unleashed and all the power of the Universe itself seems to start working for you. But it all starts with taking action.

Inspired Action vs Forced Action

Now, action, as I said, is absolutely necessary for taking your dream out of the realm of fantasy and turning it into reality. But it is important to note that there is a difference between taking inspired action and taking action to try and force something to happen. The difference between the two is critical; one will get you the results you're after and the other will just create roadblocks to make things difficult. This is an area that confuses a lot of people so, to make it clear, here's the big difference:

Forced action is action that is taken for the sole purpose of trying to make something happen. Generally speaking, it is action that you take just because you think you *should* be doing *something*.

You can tell when you're doing this type of action because it *feels* forced. There will be no excitement and no motivation for this type of action. It's going to feel like a struggle and results are going to be few and far between. Trying to take forced action is like trying to climb up a hill through a river of molasses; it's an awful lot of effort and you're not going to get very far *even though you're working really hard*. On top of that, obstacles tend to start cropping up left, right and centre and it seems like a classic one step forward, two steps back kind of scenario. You're moving and acting and doing and working... but nothing seems to actually be happening. You're spinning your wheels and getting nowhere.

Inspired action, on the other hand, is action that you take when you feel *inspired* to do it. This type of action is almost always accompanied by a rush of energy, and feelings of excitement, enthusiasm and joy.

When you're taking inspired action, you are in "the zone"; you are *flying* at high speed and everything just flows. You will accomplish more in a relatively short amount of time than you ever thought was possible. You will work harder than ever, but *it doesn't feel like work*! In fact, you might stop when you suddenly become aware that you're hungry, only to look at the clock and realize with a shock that you've completely lost track of time, and you've worked the entire day and didn't even know it! (In which case, you should definitely take a dinner break... you've earned it!)

What Inspired Action Looks Like

One of my best personal examples of inspired action happened shortly after I read Virgin Group founder and billionaire business tycoon Sir Richard Branson's autobiography, *Losing My Virginity*. Reading Branson's story inspired me to start moving forward on creating my own podcast – an idea I had been toying with for several months, but had never actually gotten around to doing anything about.

In the span of just two days, with inspired action on my side, I had researched *what* I needed to do to create a podcast, I had learned *how* to do what I needed to do, and then I actually *did* everything. I set up all the accounts I needed, I installed and figured out how to use the recording software, I recorded the raw audio files for *eighteen* episodes, and I did the sound-editing and mixing for four of those episodes *and* got them scheduled. I even created the graphics for the show, set up the RSS feed and got the podcast submitted to iTunes!

On one of those days I worked from 6:30 in the morning to 10:30 at night, but I had so much fun working that I really didn't notice how long I had been at it. On top of all of this, I even stumbled across a free webinar that helped me understand all of the things I needed to do to create a successful podcast, and I also discovered a couple of really useful online podcasting communities that provided some answers when a couple of questions cropped up. Everything just lined up perfectly!

EVERYTHING JUST FLOWS

This is the hallmark of inspired action: when you're in that zone and everything is just *flowing*, it does not feel like work; it feels like everything just magically lines up to make it happen for you, everything falls perfectly into place, and so much is accomplished.

Basically, the key difference between the two types of action is that forced action *feels* forced. It takes a long time, it is hard, it is definitely not fun, and there are very few, if any, real results to show for all your efforts. Inspired action, on the other hand, is fun, easy and joyful. There is a definite feeling of flow, and the Universe seems to go out of its way to make it all work out for you. You get massive results in relatively short timeframes, and, while you may be doing a massive amount of stuff, there is no feeling of work or effort involved. To put it even more succinctly: forced action feels *bad*, while inspired action feels *good*.

Chapter 3 Recap

❖ **Key Points to Remember:**

- We all have multiple fears in our lives. You only need to worry about are the ones that interfere with your ability to do what you most want to do.
- Commitment to your dream is critical; if you're just "interested" in it you won't do what it takes to overcome your fears and make it happen.
- Mindset and action are the two keys to working through your fears.
- Attitudes are contagious; be careful with the messages you allow yourself to be exposed to.
- You must take action in order to build your dreams. Thinking happy thoughts and watching motivational videos is not enough.

❖ **Your Action Items:**

1. Make a list of your current dreams and then make a list of specific fears that you think might be keeping you from each of these dreams. These are the important fears – the ones that you need to work on.
2. Make a list of the people, things, and situations in your life that most inspire you to be successful; the ones that motivate you to stretch yourself and keep moving toward your biggest dreams and goals. Find ways to spend more time with these people and doing these things!

❖ **Download:**

- http://www.VibeShifting.com/fearless-bonus

Chapter 4: Your Fears, Unmasked

> WE ARE AFRAID OF THE ENORMITY OF THE POSSIBLE.
> ~Emile M. Cioran, Romanian Philosopher

What if I told you that all the things that you think are preventing you from making your dreams a reality aren't really real at all? What if I told you that all those fears are the result of mistakes in the way you're thinking about your situation? In Chapter 2 you learned that fear is not real. In this chapter, we're going to take a close look at *why* all those big, insurmountable obstacles that you're despairing over are nothing more than smoke and mirrors - illusions created by your own mind.

Your mind is your most powerful asset in your quest to build your dreams. On the flip side, however, it can also be your own worst enemy, if you allow it to be. You can either harness the power of your mind to help you craft reality around the vision you have for your life, or you can allow all the scary whispers of doubt and fear to creep in, cloud that bright vision, and twist your reality into a nightmare rather than a dream. It really is your choice.

All Obstacles Can Be Overcome

I'm going to let you in on a little secret here: No obstacle is insurmountable unless you believe it is. My father, for example, had a difficult childhood. He was one of six children being raised by a divorced, alcoholic, single mother in the forties and fifties. The family was so poor that there were times when there was, literally, no food in the house. My father didn't want to spend the rest of his life like that and, even as a young man, he believed that the best way to change his life and create better circumstances for himself was to get an education. There was no way he could have afforded the cost of going to university on his own, so he joined the army because they would pay his tuition.

It doesn't matter where you're starting from; if you believe that you can achieve your goal, then you can find a way to make it happen. With enough determination and ingenuity, anything is possible... as long as you don't let your fears take hold and push you off course.

The Biology of Fear

For the purposes of this book, there are only two things you really need to know about the actual biology of fear:
1. The amygdalae[9], are small almond-shaped structures within your brain. They constantly scan the information your senses pick up for signs of danger, and when they see something they don't like they sound an alarm[10] that triggers all sorts of stress hormones to pour through your body. These are the hormones that cause

all the standard fear responses that we experience: the pounding heart, the dry mouth, the clammy hands, etc.
2. The amygdalae do not differentiate between real and imagined threats.[11]

This last point is very important, because it means that if you *think* about or *imagine* something frightening – for example, standing up to speak in front of a room full of people – your body will react to those mental cues in exactly the same way that it would to the actual, physical experience of having it happen.

Likewise, if you are constantly exposed to frightening news items about diseases, looming economic collapse, or potential terrorist threats, that threat-detection system of yours never returns to stand-by mode. In modern society, we are pretty much always on red alert mode, as far as our bodies' stress responses are concerned. (If you are interested in learning more about all of that, by the way, you can find more details in my book, *Seven-Minute Stress Busters.*)

When it comes to our dreams, this psychological aspect is by far the most important one we need to understand in order to be able to work through those fears and move forward with our dreams and goals, because fear is primarily a *cognitive* issue. It's a result of mistakes we make in how we interpret the world and the situations around us.

NEGATIVITY SPIRALS

One of the biggest cognitive mistakes we make that affects our ability to build our dreams is that we so easily get ourselves caught up in something that I call "negativity spiraling".

If you've ever had one of those days where absolutely everything seems to be going wrong – where, by the time lunch hour hits, you're just desperately wishing you'd never even gotten out of bed in the first place, you know what negativity spirals are all about. It's that snowball effect that turns one bad experience into a whole bad day, or one fearful thought into an outright panic attack.

We all have days like that once in a while, and when they happen it's hard not feel like the entire Universe is conspiring against you in some cruel campaign designed to make you as miserable as humanly possible. Unfortunately, that very feeling of victimization actually makes things worse and even perpetuates the chain of negative events unfolding around you. When these "terrible, awful, no-good, very bad days" happen they are usually a result of our own thinking and, therefore, completely preventable. Hard to swallow, isn't it? But what if it's true? What if the way we think actually affects what happens to us over the course of a day, and, by extension, the course of our entire lives?

Choose Your Own Reality

What we focus on actually does become our reality. If we have a negative experience first thing in the morning and get all bent out of shape about it, focusing on it and getting angrier and more upset about it, we are conditioning ourselves to continue interpreting other events in a negative light as well.

And the bad mood will just continue to grow and colour our interpretation of still more events in a snowball effect of misery and gloom. We start looking for more things to support our view that this is a bad day and that everything sucks, and we find them. In effect, we design and custom-build our own bad day according to our own exacting specifications through the process of focusing on negativity.

For example: You forget to set the alarm the night before so you wake up in a panic realizing you're running late (dominant thought: anxiety, "Oh no! I'm going to be late! This happened last week, too!"); then, as you tear into your bathroom for the Fastest Shower in the West you stub your toe on the door frame (dominant thought: pain, "Stupid door frame! Why do these things always happen to me? I banged my head on the cupboard door last night, and I'm always dropping the soap on my toes when I'm in the shower or getting paper cuts at work. It's not fair!").

You forgo breakfast to make a mad dash to the bus stop, only to watch in outraged disbelief as your bus pulls away from the curb, with you only 10 steps away from the door (dominant thought: victimization, "Why does everything bad always have to happen to me? Nobody ever gives me a break — bus drivers never stop for me, my boss is always giving me a hard time, and my coworkers never do their fair share!").

Fuming, you wait for the next bus, which shows up behind schedule; cursing and mumbling under your breath about how the evil power-tripping transit workers delight in making people late, you snap at the driver when you get on the bus (dominant thought: fury, "That bastard! He's late on purpose! Just like that woman at the grocery store yesterday — she took so long to ring my purchases through the cash that I didn't have time to pick up the dry cleaning! People are always going out of their way to make my life difficult!").

You finally get to your destination and take five minutes to stop and get yourself a coffee, only to have it spill down the front of your shirt when you try to take a sip because the lid wasn't on right (dominant thought: despair, ""Why does the world hate me so much? Everything always goes wrong for me! This whole day is just a mess!")

THE SNOWBALL EFFECT

Do you see how these negative thought processes work? Do you see how the spiral starts? How dwelling on one negative thought almost magnetically draws more negative thoughts to itself? How the whole process picks up speed and gets stronger with time?

Like a great big snowball, focusing on a negative thought rolls that thought over and over in your head, and packs more and more negative thoughts around that kernel, making it bigger and bigger and stronger and stronger, faster and faster, the longer you focus on it.

The problem is that once you get sucked into this kind of negativity spiral, it can be really hard to pull yourself out of it. As I said, it gets stronger the longer you stay in it. And because your thoughts affect your emotions, this is a one-way ticket to Depression-Ville and Anxiety City. You can't be in a positive mental place when you are thinking those kinds of thoughts.

What's even worse is that once the negativity takes root in your mind it affects your perception by triggering your Reticular Activating System (which we talked about in Chapter 1) to likewise focus on negativity, making it extremely difficult for you to even *see* anything that isn't likewise negative.

A CHANGE IN PERSPECTIVE

How would the scenario change, though, if, instead of the panicked leap from your bed when you realized the alarm didn't go off, you took even just two minutes to take a deep breath, change your thoughts, and say to yourself "Hey! I got a whole half-hour of extra sleep this morning! How awesome is that! Just think how much easier everything is going to be today because of it!" (dominant thought: gratitude, excitement, "Lucky me! I remember the last time I got extra sleep — I had an awesome day, and I was so on-the-ball at work that my boss actually complimented me!").

With that kind of start to your day, I bet you'd be paying more attention and therefore be less likely to stub your toe on the way to the bathroom. And I bet that on your way to the bus stop, you'd look that first bus driver right in the eye and give him a big smile, which might make him decide to wait the extra 3 seconds for you to get to the door of the bus and jump on. And so on and so forth.

Think about your dream-based fears in the same way. The more you concentrate on what scares you about your dreams, the bigger and stronger those fears will get. Shift your focus to the outcome that you want to see, however, and *that* is what you will draw energy to.

MIRROR, MIRROR...

Our world, in a very real and tangible sense, is a mirror of our own feelings and beliefs, reflecting what already exists on the inside. What we see happening around us is always interpreted through the filter of our own emotions and beliefs. Psychologists call this phenomenon *confirmation bias*. It's the tendency for human beings to look for or to interpret existing information in a way that confirms their preconceptions.[12]

In short, people tend to try to prove that what they already think is the truth. If we believe that the world is a bad place, for example, we will automatically and subconsciously look for evidence to support this belief, *and we will find it*. If we believe that the world is a good place, we will automatically and subconsciously look for evidence to support this belief, *and we will find it*. Ultimately, we get exactly what it is that we want, *whether we are consciously aware that we want it or not*.

How to Stop the Spirals

Here are four strategies that can help you make that mindset shift and put an end to negativity spirals before they start:

1. Drop the "Should"s

I think *should* is one of those words that we'd all be better off dropping from our vocabularies. *Should* is an extremely judgemental word; by its very nature it says that we're not good enough, that we haven't measured up to some kind of standard. But who gets to decide what those standards are? When it comes to our dreams, an awful lot of the *shoulds* we place on ourselves are really arbitrary; who says we should have something done in a particular time frame, or in a certain way, or only by following a particular path? Why should anyone else – individual or society – get to have that kind of power over *your* life?

So when you catch yourself using *should*, either out loud or in the silence of your own mind, try replacing it with something like *could*. In other words, "I should get this article done today" becomes "I could get this article done today". It may seem like a minor shift, but there's an energy attached to the meaning behind those words, and even a small shift like that can have a big impact.

2. Don't Compare Yourself to Others

This is a big one. And we're all guilty of doing it; we all compare ourselves to other people. We see how other people are managing to do what we are currently only dreaming of and we can't, for the life of us, figure out how to get from here to there. So we assume there must be something wrong with us, or that we somehow lack the ability to make it happen. But the far more likely reality is simply that those others are just further ahead in their journey than we are. We're comparing our boring concrete foundational structure to their glitzy, completed castle, and that's just not a fair comparison.

So don't compare yourself to anyone else. Focus instead on your own journey, and on taking the small, really unglamorous but critically important steps that are the foundation of what it is that *you* want to build.

3. Let the Past Go

We spend so much of our time beating ourselves up over things that have happened in the past. But to what end? No amount of self-recrimination is going to change what happened or what didn't happen. We cannot change the past, and anything we plan for the future is hypothetical. The only moment over which we have any control at all is what happens in the now. Our power lies in the present moment; always and only.

Mindfulness is a powerful tool for peace of mind, so do your best to practice it whenever you can. Your ability to remain grounded in the present will become stronger the more you do it.

4. Use Your Vibe Shifters

You do have a go-to list of things that help to snap you

out of the occasional funk, right? *Right?* If not, make one. Now. Here are a few suggestions to get you started:

- Hit iTunes and create a playlist of upbeat songs that always cheer you up, and if you can't think of any, I've got a couple of playlists on my YouTube channel[13] that can get you started.
- Create a scrapbook or Pinterest board of inspirational quotes that remind you of who you are and what you're trying to accomplish in life; quotes that motivate you to get yourself back on track. Again, if you don't know where to start, you can check out my Pinterest boards[14] for inspiration!
- Find a hobby that allows you to de-stress and focus on something creative instead of the distressing thoughts flooding through your mind: painting, reading, dance, gardening, whatever; just find something and start doing it.
- Create a mantra that you can repeat to yourself to regain your balance when you start feeling off-kilter.

In short, do whatever you need to do to shift yourself out of that bad-feeling mind-space and into something better.

A MATTER OF CHOICE

Getting stuck in a negative mood is the first step in a negativity spiral that leads to frustration, depression and anxiety. The longer you stay in that kind of mindset, the stronger it gets and the harder it is for you to break free of it.

Make it a point to change your own internal dialogue, and you will begin to change your experience of the world around you. If you choose to deliberately focus on good thoughts and feelings, you will then start to see good things in the world around you that generate even more good feelings. It's all a matter of choice.

The Genie in the Bottle

So we've just let the genie out of the bottle; you now know what your own mind is capable of, so how does it make you feel? Now that you know how powerful your thoughts are and how they can shape not only your day, but your entire life, does the idea of being the absolute creator of your own reality empower you or frighten you?

Sometimes, when people start learning about how much control they really have over the outside world, instead of getting excited about the possibilities, they go the other way and start getting scared. They become deathly afraid of every negative thought that crosses their minds, and absolutely terrified that if they can't control their thoughts, terrible things will start to happen.

It's Not Pandora's Box

I received an email once from a very upset reader who believed that she had "opened Pandora's Box" in learning about how much her own mind affected things. She was certain that her negative thoughts, which now terrified her, were causing chaos in her life.

In Greek mythology, legend had it that Pandora's Box was an artifact containing all the evils of the world. But there is no evil in this. You're not opening yourself up to some mystical, dangerous power when you learn this stuff – these principles have *always* been working in your life, whether you've been aware of them or not, and they will always *continue* to work in your life, whether you choose to acknowledge them or not. Far better to learn how they work and then use that knowledge in your favour, don't you think?

Focus on the good – on what you want to see and create and experience. And remember that the magic exists *within* you; it has *always* been a part of you and always will be. You just have to decide what to do with it. And rest assured that there are ways to cope with your negative thoughts, and that you are not going to destroy your life if you can't immediately put an end to them.

What to Do If Your Thoughts Scare You

When you start panicking over your negative thoughts and what they could be manifesting into your life, just stop. Stop, take a deep breath, and remind yourself that the system is stacked in your favour – there is an unbreakable safety net built into our existence here. Think of all the times things have looked bad in your life, and realize that you're still here and still standing. Despite everything that you have already been through, your track record for survival right now is 100%, and there is a reason for that: the system is skewed to work in your best interests!

The whole process is set up to magnify your positive thoughts and minimize your negative ones. When you start consciously looking at your negative thoughts and realizing just how many of them you have in a day (we'll talk about that more in Chapter 9), this fact should become obvious. If you've been running that automated negative programming for so long, and are still managing to manifest *anything* positive into your life, then you *know* that you are much better at creating positive things than you are at creating negative things.

Your positive thoughts are far more powerful than your negative thoughts, so when you start getting scared, grab onto that. Just let the negative thoughts pass, and reach for better-feeling ones. You're not going to be an expert at this stuff right away — none of us are. But you keep trying. And it does get easier. And soon, you're going to start seeing evidence of how quickly you're able to manifest the good things.

CHOOSE LOVE OR CHOOSE FEAR

If you see the power of your own mind as something to punish you for not being strong enough to control them, and if your fears about your own abilities are running rampant through your mind, it's not a wonder that the situations you create in your physical world would be less than ideal. When you're focused on fear and negativity that is what the dominant flavour of your experiences in life will involve.

Let's go Disney for a moment and think about Queen Elsa, from the movie *Frozen*. She spent a lifetime being terrified of her own power. She hid herself away in her room for years and refused to have anything to do with the outside world. She was so afraid of hurting anyone. But the more afraid she became of her power, the more out-of-control it became; she was so focused on fear that all she could create were more situations that caused fear.

It was not until Elsa realized that *love* was the answer. Once she chose love instead of fear, she realized just how easy it was to control her power and use it to build positive experiences. She realized how much fun it could be, how much beauty she could create with it, and how much joy that power could bring, not only to herself, but to all the people of her kingdom.

When you strip away all the window dressing, all the fluff, and all the things that you think are "complications", every single choice in your life comes down to that choice between love or fear. It's a deliberate choice, and one that will have a profound impact on your life from here on in.

You can choose to live in love and focus on the beautiful vision that you see inside of you, allowing *that* to be the dominant creative power in your life, or you can choose to let fear take the lead. It's up to you.

Primary vs Secondary Fears

If you're like most people you have a lot of fears; some of them conscious, many of them subconscious. We all do, and that's just part of being human. But the funny thing about our fears is that so many of the ones that have the biggest impact on how we live our lives aren't really our own; they're fears we've picked up from our associations with other people. And most of those second-hand, or *secondary*, fears find their roots in the situations in which we grew up — we picked them up as children, from our parents and our families.

I use the term "secondary fears" to refer to the fears and blocks that we have picked up from other people, as opposed to fears that we have picked up through direct personal experience. As a simple example, a primary fear would be my own fear of spiders that developed after waking up one morning as a child to see one dangling in the air directly over my face and then having it drop right on my pillow the second I leaped, terrified, out of bed. A secondary fear would be my daughter's fear of spiders because she's seen my reaction to the horrible things, even though she, herself, has never had a traumatic experience with one.

WHERE YOUR FEARS COME FROM

I most often notice secondary fears in people around the topics of money, and by extension, career choices. For a lot of us, there were acceptable career choices and there were unacceptable career choices, even as young children.

For example, when I was little and wanted to be a roboticist and a veterinarian, my father was approving and supportive of those choices, but when I wanted to be a singer and an artist I was told that yes, I had plenty of talent and singing/drawing would be a nice hobby, but that "no one ever makes any money at it" and that there was "a reason for the phrase *starving artist*".

Even though, at my young age, he would have known that I would be highly likely to change my mind many times before finally embarking on my ultimate career path, there were already limitations put on which paths were acceptable and which were not. And these limitations centred on whether or not, *in his opinion*, the routes I was considering were likely to be safe, secure and reasonably well-paying.

From my earliest memories, I was always encouraged to follow an academic path in math, science or engineering, even though I had little interest in them. But I did it because that's what my dad said I should.

I never took drama or music after grade school, even though I loved both subjects, and I dropped art after getting my mandatory two credits in high school. I filled up my schedule with all the maths (which I hated) and all the sciences and only took the minimum required business credits (which I actually really enjoyed). Because that's what I had been taught that sensible people did.

Your Parents' Beliefs

Now, my dad grew up in a very poor family (as I mentioned before, his family was so poor that they sometimes had nothing to eat). So his views about job security and money and all his fears surrounding those issues came from that childhood and growing up in that kind of poverty.

He believed without doubt that education was the key to getting out of that cycle and building a better life for himself – and for him, it was. He was the only one in his family to continue his education after high school, and the only way he was able to do it was to join the army and have them pay his tuition with the promise that he would continue working for them after graduating.

For my father, a degree in engineering was the way out of that cycle of poverty, and math and science were things he placed on a pedestal as the only really worthwhile career options.

But, thanks to my dad's life choices, I never grew up like that. I never worried about money or lack of anything else while growing up. Whenever I'd complain about there being nothing to eat in the house, it was because there was nothing in the house that I particularly felt like eating, but there was always food in the house and I was *never* hungry. And I always had everything I needed in life; not having the basics was just not in my realm of experience.

My experience was so different from my father's that there was no need for me to have the same kind of money fears he did because I started off so much further ahead than he did. But, because I was exposed to his fears and points of view for so long, and from such a young age, I picked them up anyway.

Realizing that my beliefs and fears about money and "acceptable" career choices came from my father was really an "ah-ha" moment for me. It made me realize that my unconsciously adopted fears were having a big impact on my life choices, with detrimental effects on my happiness and experience of life. I needed to let go of these fears in order to be able to move ahead with my *own* life, rather than living something that was a kind of shadow of what I thought my dad would want.

A GIFT TO THE WORLD

Most parents just want their children to be happy, and a lot of the pressure they put on their kids comes from their own fears about what is considered acceptable and safe. They are afraid that if their children make the wrong decisions, that they will suffer for it and be unhappy, so they try to get them to do what *they* think the right thing should be.

But children are not, and cannot be their parents. And trying to mould children into what you think they should be just invalidates what they already are, and that, in the end, is what causes the most suffering for those children. Because what they already are – what *you* already are – is such an incredible, wonderful gift to the world; that unique spark is here for a *reason* and trying to change it is just... wrong.

Worse, it deprives the world of that bit of irreplaceable magic that each individual child is here to contribute. Far better it is to support our children in the journey of discovering what their unique gifts are and helping them to find their own unique ways of sharing those gifts with the world.

Your Life is Waiting...

As a child, you can't really help but be influenced by the beliefs of your parents; when you are small, your existence depends on the people who provide you with the necessities of life. Your family is the single biggest influence on your own thought patterns and belief systems, whether you're aware of it or not. And your parents' fears had a huge impact on the way in which they raised you.

But thanks in large part to their own efforts to make things better for you, you're not starting off from the same place that they did. You were born in another time and in a whole different world than the one in which your parents grew up in, and where their fears might have been a survival tool for them, all they do for you is hold you back from living your own life on your own terms.

Learn to recognize the secondary fears that you've picked up along the way, and then let them go. Your life is waiting!

The Four Most Common Dream-Killing Fears

Now that you know where most of your fears have come from, it's time to get acquainted with the most common dream-killing fears out there. And these fears, as we mentioned at the beginning of the book, are:

1. The fear of failure;
2. The fear of success;
3. The fear of judgement; and,
4. The fear of the unknown

That's it – just four basic fears that are the most likely to keep you from turning your own dreams into reality.

In the next four chapters, we're going to take a close look at each one of these fears individually so that you can get really clear about how they work and how they affect you. We're also going to look at specific strategies that you can take for each type of fear that will help you get through them and get back on track to creating the kind of success that you most want for yourself.

Each fear has its own unique markers, but all the fears are in some way based on the final fear: the fear of the unknown. This is the biggie; this is the fear that, in some way, shape, or form, lies at the heart of each of the other dream-killing fears. This is the core fear that keeps us from doing everything that we know we need to do in order to create the extraordinary and turn our biggest dreams into our actual reality.

Chapter 4 Recap

❖ *Key Points to Remember:*

- Your brain does not distinguish between real and imagined fear. Your body will respond to an actual threat and an imagined threat in exactly the same way.
- Negativity spirals occur when we focus on a minor negative event and cause it to snowball into a major negative experience.
- Your own mind is phenomenally powerful in shaping your external reality and experience of life, but this is not something to be afraid of; the system is skewed in favour of the positive.
- Secondary fears are the fears that you have picked up over time from other people, rather than through your own direct experience.

❖ *Your Action Items:*

1. Review the strategies for stopping negativity spirals on page 66 and be sure to use them next time you feel yourself on the edge of a spiral.
2. Make a list of the secondary fears that you have picked that may be impacting your ability to build your dreams and create your extraordinary life.

❖ *Download:*

- http://www.VibeShifting.com/fearless-bonus

Chapter 5:
The Fear of Failure

> ONLY THOSE WHO DARE TO FAIL GREATLY
> CAN EVER ACHIEVE GREATLY.
> ~Robert F. Kennedy, Former American Senator

Sometimes you look at an opportunity that lies before you and, for a moment, the excitement of *possibility* courses through you; you feel alive and almost giddy with the thought of everything you could do. And then the doubts creep in.

You start to wonder if maybe that golden opportunity is too good to be true. You think there has to be a catch somewhere. And then you start to think that maybe you're not ready for it yet, that maybe it's beyond your current capabilities. Then you start to get scared; what if you can't pull it off? What if you give it your best shot but you mess it up anyway? So then you start to panic; what if you *fail* and make an absolute fool of yourself and everyone laughs at you and says "I told you so"?

You've decided, before you've even taken the first tiny step forward, that it won't work. Before you've even begun, you've doomed yourself to failure. Don't beat yourself up over it – it happens to everyone at some point in their journey. The loss of a specific opportunity isn't the concern here; the bigger issue is the reason behind why you let it go: for some, the fear that we might fail is enough to make us never start.

In reality, though, failure is really not such a bad thing; it can help us to improve on an original idea; it can help us to realize that we need to head in a different direction; it can even act as a magical force that allows us to realize previously unknown reserves of strength and determination that steel us to do whatever we need to in order to succeed.

Yes, failure can hurt. It bruises the ego a whole awful lot and this can make a lot of people want to shut down their dreams to avoid risking further pain. What would happen, though, if you tried to shift your perspective a little? What if, instead of viewing failure as a calamity, you started to think of it as just another part of the plan; a normal part of the *process* that is success?

With this view, failure is actually seen as a *good* thing because it means you're out there *doing* something! Think about it for a moment: the only people who never fail are those who never even make the attempt to do anything with their lives!

Famous "Failures"

British industrial designer James Dyson, the inventor of the Dyson sphere vacuum cleaner, created 5127 prototypes[15] of his famous vacuum cleaner between 1979 and 1984, before finally finding a design that worked — and even then no one was interested in it! It wasn't until his vacuum cleaner won an award in Japan in 1991 that interest in Dyson's invention began to grow. Today, Dyson is billion-dollar company employing thousands of people around the world, and pretty much everyone has at least heard of the Dyson vacuum cleaner.

American singer-songwriter Rachel Platten was launched into international super-stardom when her multi-platinum-award-winning pop anthem "Fight Song" seemingly appeared out of nowhere in the fall of 2015. But, in reality, she had been working hard for twelve years[16], driving around the country in her mother's SUV and playing any gig she could get in an effort to generate interest in her music, before "Fight Song" hit the iTunes top 100 and became an inspirational battle cry for everyone from Ford Motors to individuals battling cancer.

British author J.K. Rowling had the idea for *Harry Potter* in mind and then suffered a string of tragic events: the death of her mother; an abusive relationship in a foreign country that ended in a divorce that left her as a single parent to an infant; she returned to England with her baby and not much else, ending up on welfare in order to feed her child; all of which no doubt contributed to her diagnosis of clinical depression. And then after all of this, her book, *Harry Potter and the Philosopher's Stone*, was rejected by *twelve* publishers before finally being picked up by Bloomsbury (who still told her she'd better get a day job because the book wouldn't amount to much).

The Harry Potter series, of course, went on to become the fastest selling books in history[17] and, as of 2015, the brand is now worth an estimated fifteen billion dollars world-wide.

Failure is Part of the Process

The point of these stories is that the success of these individuals came after many *failures*. And the reason that Dyson and Platten and Rowling, and all of the others like them, eventually succeeded is that *they didn't give up*. They were persistent. They didn't let their failures define them or defeat them — they used them as stepping stones to create the visions they believed in. They worked their tails off, of course, but they believed in themselves, they learned from every mistake they made, and they poured everything they had into making it happen. They did not quit trying just because of the pain they experienced from failing in their initial attempts.

And that's the real issue when it comes to all of this: the worst part of failure is that it *hurts* us. It makes us feel badly about *ourselves*, and brings out all of the ugliest emotions we have: fear; embarrassment; humiliation; anger. And for a lot of people, this awful mish-mash of unpleasant feelings becomes so uncomfortable; it shakes their identity to such an extent that they give up, rather than having to deal with it, or risk experiencing it again.

But for successful individuals, failure is viewed as part of the process. They learn to deal with the emotional aftermath when things go wrong, and in learning from failure it becomes a catalyst, spurring them ever-onward towards their dreams.

So keep an open mind when it comes to your failures. Realize that just because something you *did* failed, it does not mean that *you* are a failure. Use the experience to create an even better version of what you had originally planned and let it renew your determination to succeed. In learning from failure you can, to paraphrase J.K. Rowling, take what you thought was rock bottom and turn into the foundation for the rest of your life.

PERMISSION TO MAKE MISTAKES

Also remember that you don't have to do something perfectly in order to do it well, and that if you never *try* anything new, you'll never *do* anything new, either. It takes a certain amount of risk and a certain amount of fear to build the extraordinary; big dreams never get built in people's comfort zones, and if you want to achieve great things in your life, you have to realize that you won't be great at it right out of the gate. No one is. You learn from experience, as you go along.

You have to give yourself permission to make mistakes and be a beginner. You have to be willing to let go of perfectionism and let yourself be bad at something. You have to be willing to completely suck at it... because how else are you going to learn? You have to be willing to fall flat on your face and then pick yourself up and keep going, as many times as it takes, because that's when real success happens.

PERFECTIONISM IS A BAD HABIT

Perfectionism is one of those things I used to struggle with constantly. When I did things, I wanted to know that I had done them to the best of my ability, and I had no tolerance for slip-ups. When I messed up on something that I really wanted to do, I was *very* hard on myself. And it really wasn't a healthy personality trait to have, because you're constantly in a state of stress if you feel like you never measure up to your own standards.

This perfectionist habit of mine held me back from doing so many things, because I didn't want to do them unless I knew that I could do them well; I did not want to try something that I knew I would just screw up, and it was only after a rather horrible ego-bashing experience I had early on in my Toastmasters' career that I learned to let it go; to start accepting my failures as the learning experiences they were, and to start seeing my screw-ups with a touch of humour, rather than the soul-crushing embarrassment they used to hold over me.

When You Fail in Front of a Crowd

According to Wikipedia, "perfectionism... is a personality trait characterized by a person's striving for flawlessness and setting excessively high performance standards, accompanied by overly critical self-evaluations and concerns regarding others' evaluations."[18]

This definition really hit home for me after a particularly disastrous second speech that I gave for my Toastmasters group. It was awful. I had memorized the speech, practised and polished it until it shone; it had a great opening and was even kind of funny... and when I stood up in front of that room I got about three sentences into it and then froze. I could not remember a single word of the speech I had so carefully prepared.

I struggled my way through, and everybody was really nice in the evaluations, mentioning all the things they liked about the speech. And all I could concentrate on was how awful I'd been. I could not see *any* good points to my performance at all.

I actually cried when I got home because I was so mad at myself for screwing up so badly, and I was upset for two whole days, which was ridiculous, because Toastmasters is all about *learning*. It's a totally non-threatening environment in which to practice and become more comfortable speaking in front of an audience.

SHAKE IT OFF...

That experience was kind of a crossroads for me. I could have hung my head in shame, continued beating myself up over my failure and given up on Toastmasters altogether (because, obviously, I was terrible at it). Or I could pick myself up, shake it all off, and try again another day (because one bad speech does not a bad speaker make).

I picked the second route.

For perfectionists – and most people, I've discovered, are perfectionists to one extent or another – it's hard not to be hard on yourself when you don't measure up to your own standards. We all want to be good at what we most want to do, but if we let our fear of failure and our desire to be *perfect* prevent us from acquiring the experience we need in order to be *excellent*, then we'll never even get out of the gate.

How to Let Go of Perfectionism

So with that in mind, here are some of the strategies that I used to get over the perfectionist habits that were allowing my fear of failure to keep me from achieving my own goals:

1. Find One Good Thing You Did Right

You may feel your performance was awful in every regard, but there is always at least one thing you did right or did well. Look for it, and you will find it; it's always there.

2. JUST STOP

Stop beating yourself up. Actually tell yourself: "Stop!" as soon as you become aware of the negative self-talk you're subjecting yourself to. Remind yourself that it's not the end of the world just because it didn't go as planned. You *know* you'll do better next time, so don't sweat it now.

3. BE A BETTER FRIEND

If you had a friend who talked to you the same way you talk to yourself, you'd drop 'em like yesterday's garbage. Think about what a good friend would say to you, or what you would say to your best friend if he or she was in your shoes. Give yourself some encouragement!

4. ADJUST YOUR STANDARDS

If your standards are higher for yourself than they are for anyone else, then that should probably tell you something; perhaps your standards are just plain unrealistic. What would your reaction be if someone else had just performed the same way you did? If you would be supportive of them and happy for what they did well, then you should have those same standards for yourself.

5. MOVE ON

These things happen sometimes; let it be and let it go. Ask yourself what you can learn from what happened and what one thing you can concentrate on to improve your next attempt. Then take one step forward at a time, and don't give up.

Perfectionism can be a difficult habit to break, but leaving this habit unchecked can have very detrimental effects on your ability to build your dreams. Things don't always go as planned, but like I said before – things don't have to be perfect in order to be good, or even great!

Turning Your Doubts into Stepping Stones

Doubt is a normal part of the process when we start working towards our dreams. Everyone feels doubt, but getting past your doubts is critical to getting anywhere in life. Unfortunately, figuring out how, exactly, to conquer those doubts is sometimes easier said than done. Because doubts can be powerful, frightening things that make us question everything about ourselves, our decisions and our dreams themselves.

The key to getting past your doubts is to find ways of bringing these half-hidden fears into the open and shining a light onto them so you can really see them for what they are; so that you can understand that they are nothing that you can't easily handle; so that you can finally shake off their grip and realize that they have no power over you.

Here is a process that you can use to help you shine that light on your fears:

Step 1: Acknowledge the Doubt

The first thing to do is to acknowledge the fact that you have the doubt or the fear in the first place. Don't wallow in it, of course, but acknowledge the fact that it's there. Write the specific doubt or fear down on paper so you can see it. This helps to externalize the doubt rather than have it continue lurking around in your subconscious, ready to sabotage you when you least expect it.

Most of our doubts and fears are really just phantoms – they seem bigger and scarier than they really are because they are half-hidden in the shadows of our own minds. Partially seen, partially hidden, but always there and always unsettling. Kind of like the bogeyman in the closet or the monster lurking under a child's bed.

When you bring the doubts out of your head and onto paper, it has the effect of turning the light on to banish the monster – you can see the shadow for what it *really* is, rather than the scary monster your mind has built it up to be. The doubt is reduced in size and complexity, and the locus of power shifts away from it and back into your own sphere of control.

STEP 2: GET PERSPECTIVE

Now I want you to take a good, hard look at that doubt. And I want you to ask yourself what the worst thing that could happen is, should that doubt or fear actually be realized. Really think about this, and answer the question honestly. Because for most of us, and in almost every single case, the worst possible outcome is never as bad as we're afraid it might be.

For example, if you're afraid a new career or business venture might fail, what's the worst that could happen? You lose your income and your house? You'll find a new job, sooner or later, and in the meantime you might have to ask family or friends for temporary help or a place to stay. But you would get through it and survive.

Likewise, if you're afraid that a romantic relationship with the person you're head over heels for will fail, what's the worst that could happen? You get dumped, you're heartbroken, and you spend a week hiding in bed listening to depressing music with the curtains drawn and the covers pulled over your head. And then you'll pull yourself together, move on, and eventually find someone better. Whatever the worst possible outcome is, by acknowledging that thought and realizing that, no matter what, you *will* find a way to get through it, the fear immediately loses a lot of its power.

STEP 3: CREATE CONTINGENCY PLANS

Ask yourself what could possibly go wrong? Make a list of all those fears. Now figure out what you're going to do IF any of those things happen. In any bad situation, there's always *something* that can be done to improve it.

Figuring out what you're going to do in each of your hypothetical situations, before any of them ever happen, will help you to stop worrying about them because you'll have a script or action plan in place to tell you exactly what to do if ever you find yourself in any of those situations.

STEP 4: REALIZE THAT YOU ARE NOT ALONE

Realize that all of your doubts and fears have also been experienced by others – *you are not alone.* Most doubts and fears boil down to feeling like you're not good enough. And this is something that *all* people deal with from time to time. But while successful people *feel* the fear, they do not allow it to *control* them. Acknowledge your fear, but follow your dream anyway.

STEP 5: BE HERE NOW

Many of our doubts and fears are caused by us ignoring the present moment and focusing ourselves in either the future or the past. Reliving past failures and traumas only leads to depression. Fearing what *might* happen in the future only leads to anxiety and panic attacks. Living in the *now*, the present moment, allows you to fully live your life as it is. There is no berating yourself for the perceived mistakes of the past, and no needless worry about dramas that may never even come to pass.

When you find yourself drifting into worry or regret, recognize that you have shifted your focus out of your *now*, and gently bring your awareness back to the present. Focus yourself on your plan and, as Theodore Roosevelt, the 26th President of the United States once said, just "do what you can, with what you have, from where you are". It will *always* be enough.

STEP 6: LET IT BE AND LET IT GO

Let go of the doubt and the fear - you don't need it any more. So I want you to take that paper from step 1, where you wrote down your doubt. Read it over one more time. Then crumple it up and stomp on it, or shred it into tiny pieces or (very carefully and in a safe location and manner) burn it. Destroy that paper, and your fear along with it. Release the fear and the doubt into the hands of the Universe - it's more than willing and more than capable of handling it for you, so allow it to do so. Let the fear go, and trust that it's being taken care of.

This step frees you to focus on your successes. Every time something goes right or you make even the smallest progress towards your goal, celebrate it! Focus on the good things and feel the joy and excitement in them! This will pave the way for even greater success to come your way.

BREAKING THE WORRY HABIT

Worrying about failure is one of those double-edged swords; on the one hand, a little bit of worrying can be helpful, in the sense that it can keep you alert and on your toes, and spur you on to take action that could actually help you to avoid negative situations. But on the other hand, too much worrying can really have a detrimental effect on both your mental and physical health. Figuring out when that line between "a little bit" and "too much" gets crossed and learning how to stop worrying when you want to is critical to keeping yourself focused on building your biggest dreams.

WHEN IS WORRYING A PROBLEM?

If your worrying is short-lived, kicks you into action to solve a problem, and then subsides when the specific problem is dealt with, then you're OK. But if your worrying is chronic and you find yourself constantly going over "what-if" scenarios and imagining the worst possible outcome to any situation, then worrying is a problem. Unchecked worrying of the latter sort can cause your anxiety levels to soar, locking you into a negativity spiral of self-doubt, fear, and even outright depression. It's hard to feel good about your life when you're always thinking about doomsday possibilities to everything!

Fortunately, worrying is just another mental habit. And habits can be changed. So with that in mind, here are three strategies that you can start using today to help you make that change:

STRATEGY #1: DISTRACT YOURSELF

When you realize that a worrying thought has taken hold of you, distract yourself with something else. Get busy working on your "to-do" list of stuff you know you can actually do something about; put that worrying energy to good use and get stuff done! Alternatively, call a friend, watch a funny movie or read a book. Try listening to some upbeat music to help shift yourself into a better feeling mood. Just do something (anything!) that will shift your focus onto something other than what you're worrying about.

STRATEGY #2: FIND STILLNESS

It seems that every moment of our waking lives is filled up with *stuff* these days. We're constantly doing things – we're on our smart phones, we're checking our email, we're surfing the Internet, we're reading, we're watching, we're listening, we're talking... we are *always* distracted by *something*. But when we can find ourselves moments of stillness and silence, the space to just breathe and be... this stillness has a powerful ability to reconnect us with our centre and allow us to hear that voice within once again.

STRATEGY #3: IMAGINE A HAPPY ENDING

If there is a particular problem that has you in a knot, then use the power of your own mind and visualize the outcome that you would most like to see. Instead of worrying about all the bad possibilities, focus on what the best possible outcome would be – get detailed and put yourself in the picture. Focus on that happy ending and *believe* that this is what *will* happen.

Allowing your worry and fears about potential failure to run wild can actually prevent you from ever getting started on your dreams. Learning how to stop the mental habits that create chronic worrying with will help you get back on track to success.

IF YOU WANT TO GET GOOD, YOU MUST GET STARTED

American author and motivational speaker Zig Ziglar once said that "You don't have to be great to start, but you have to start to be great." I love this quote because I think a lot of people hold themselves back from getting started on things that are important to them because they're afraid that they won't be good enough. They're afraid that if they take a shot at something that means the world to them, they'll fail and be devastated.

DON'T COMPARE YOURSELF TO OTHERS

Once I got over my perfectionist habit and started getting good with my public speaking, I began volunteering to give impromptu (improvised, on-the-spot, full-length speeches) at my Toastmasters club when there were empty spots in the speaking schedule. And I was talking to someone one day after having done one of those speeches and he told me that he had been watching some of the guests and new members while I was speaking, and that it had been fascinating to watch their expressions move from rapt attention to outright terror. And I was horrified – it was supposed to be an inspirational speech, not something to scare people!

The gentleman quickly reassured me that it had, indeed been a highly inspirational speech, but he said that he could just see on their faces exactly what they were thinking – they were looking at me up there at the front of the room and they were thinking "Oh no... what have I gotten myself into? Is this what's expected in Toastmasters? I could never do that! I could never go up there and speak like that!"

And I looked at him in surprise and disbelief for a minute as he was telling me this, and then I just burst out laughing. Because the thing is, two years earlier, when I first started with Toastmasters, I could never have done a speech like that either. Not to save my life; not even as something prepared and rehearsed, let alone an off-the cuff, improvised thing like that speech had been.

And I just kept thinking: if only those newbies could have seen the early days. My first speeches where I stood huddled behind the lectern, clinging to it like the life preserver it was, because it was the only way to hide the terrified shaking of my hands.

If only they knew what it had cost me, what I went through, every single time I made myself sign up to speak. The panic attacks; the sledgehammer pounding of my heart in my chest, the sudden Sahara-dryness of my mouth that made it almost impossible to speak at all, the almost certain feeling that I was either going to pass out or throw up... *every single time I got up in front of that room to speak.*

If only those newbies could have seen the history: that worst speech that I ever gave, where I forgot everything; all the mistakes that I'd made; all the *experience* that had to be accrued before that impromptu speech could have become even the most remote of *possibilities* for me.

If only they could have seen all of that, then maybe they wouldn't be so scared.

THE REAL KEY TO SUCCESS

We have this tendency as human beings to view success as a straight line from point A to point B. We assume that those who are successful – in particular, those are already doing well what we most want to be doing ourselves – we assume that they just made a decision one day and were like rock stars from the very beginning. But that's not the way it works. There is no such thing as an overnight success. It doesn't happen. Not ever.

As you learned in Chapter 3, seemingly sudden success stories, in reality, usually only happen after years of dedicated effort and many failed attempts. We see Point A and we see Point B but we rarely see what happened between the two. It's like there's a black box in between those points, hiding the whole process from us.

But if you could pop the lid off that box and look inside, you would see that success is anything but a straight line. It's more a like a tangled maze of twists and turns and ups and downs, and a whole lot of backtracking from the dead ends of things tried and failed.

And it's only when you become aware of all of that – when you can see what was *really* involved – that it becomes obvious what the real key to success, in public speaking or in any area of your life, truly is. And that key is *persistence*; successful people don't give up. They don't view failure as a final curtain call; they view it as just another twist in the maze. They chalk it up to experience, learn whatever they can from it, and then they move on and try again. They don't let fear, frustration, or wounded pride give them an excuse to quit.

Do the Scary Things

Successful people, in other words, are willing to make mistakes, and they are willing to persistently push themselves out of their comfort zones if they believe it will help them get closer to where they want to be. If J.K. Rowling had given up after the first eleven rejection letters, there would be no

Harry Potter. If George Lucas had given up after nineteen years of limited success, there would be no *Star Wars*. If the Wright Brothers had given up after the first six years of failed attempts, they would never have built the world's first flying airplane.[19]

It was American author and motivational speaker Jack Canfield who once said: "Don't worry about failures, worry about the chances you miss when you don't even try."

So I would like to encourage you to fail. I would like to encourage you to make mistakes and to be persistent in doing the things that scare you over and over again, until they don't scare you anymore. Because that is how you will find *your* key to success.

Chapter 5 Recap

- ❖ *Key Points to Remember:*
    - A habit of perfectionism is usually just fear of failure in disguise.
    - Getting through your self-doubt involves bringing your half-hidden fears out of the dark corners of your mind and into your conscious awareness.
    - Worrying is a double-edged sword; a little bit keeps you on your toes, but too much can grind your dreams to a halt.
    - Success is not a straight line. Be prepared for repeated failures and learn to embrace them as a normal part of the *process* of success.

- ❖ *Your Action Items:*
    1. Review the strategies for overcoming perfectionism on page 85.
    2. Complete the 6-step process for turning your doubts into stepping stones on page 87.
    3. Review the tips for dealing with too much worrying on page 91.

- ❖ *Download:*
    - http://www.VibeShifting.com/fearless-bonus

Chapter 6: The Fear of Success

> Our deepest fear is not that we are inadequate.
> Our deepest fear is that we are powerful beyond measure.
> ~Marianne Williamson, American Spiritual Teacher, Author and Lecturer

In the previous chapter we talked about the fear of failure. But for some people, it's not failure that scares them most, but the fear that they will *succeed*. And while the fear of success is actually one of the most common fears out there, it's a concept that seems counter-intuitive on the surface because, really, don't we all *want* our dreams to come true?

On a conscious level the answer, of course would be "yes", but the really interesting thing about this particular fear is that most people aren't even aware that that's what they're dealing with; being afraid to succeed is almost always an *unconscious* thing. And this can make it particularly difficult to deal with, because it has to be brought forth into your conscious mind — you have to become consciously aware of the fact that you have it — before you can actually begin to do anything about it.

Why Would Anyone Fear Success?

There are many facets to the fear of success, the most common of which involve the subconscious beliefs that:

- success will somehow alter who we are in a way that we won't like;
- we won't be able to handle all the changes, responsibilities, and potential downsides that come with success;
- other people won't like us anymore and we'll lose our connections with those who are important to us if we become successful;
- we'll be found out as "frauds" because we don't feel like we have our own lives together enough and, therefore, don't deserve to be successful.

In looking at these beliefs, you can see that fear of success almost always arises because, on some level, we think that the bad parts about being successful in our goals will outweigh the good parts (and there are always going to be both good and not-so-good changes resulting from our success).

If your subconscious mind is focused on what it sees as the not-so-good consequences of your success, then you will be relentlessly, but unconsciously, sabotaging yourself so that you don't succeed (and therefore you won't have to suffer the not-so-good stuff).

Success Means Change

As American motivational speaker Dennis Waitley once said, "success can be heavy"; it carries a burden with it, and it means that things are *going* to change. If we are successful with our goals, our lives will change, and not all of those changes are going to be ones that we like. That's just the way it is sometimes. And if our fears about the potential changes that could result from our success outweigh our belief in the benefit of those changes, then our self-protection mechanisms kick in and we just won't allow ourselves to manifest that success. And the bigger the dream or the goal (and therefore the bigger the potential changes), the bigger this effect is likely to be.

YOUR BELIEFS AFFECT YOUR ABILITY TO SUCCEED

For example, if your goal is to become fabulously wealthy, you might be consciously focused on what you think the good part of that is (it would be fun, you'd be able to shop whenever you want and never worry about money, etc.) but your subconscious mind might be thinking about the bad parts (ingrained beliefs that rich people are "bad" and you don't want to be a bad person, you wouldn't know who your real friends were versus those who just liked you for your money, you really have no idea how to look after massive amounts of wealth properly, etc.)

If your subconscious mind feels that the possibility of wealth and fortune suddenly turning you into an arrogant, self-obsessed jerk who will be hated by everyone you've ever known outweighs the potential fun of being able to jet-set around the world in your private airplane, then you are not going to succeed in your goal. It doesn't matter whether you would *actually* turn into that jerk or not, it's what you *believe* on that subconscious level that matters. It's that *belief* that impacts your reality.

DO YOU HAVE A FEAR OF SUCCESS?

So that's where fear of success comes from. But if all of this is happening at a subconscious level, then how can you know if it's something that you're actually dealing with? Fortunately, there are a number of telling behaviours that can indicate fear of success in disguise, such as:

- Never actually completing a project or achieving a goal (although you might be working madly towards a lot of them all at once)
- Frequently doubting yourself, your abilities, the quality of your work, or the worthiness of your dreams
- Constantly procrastinating or talking more about what you're *planning* to do rather than what you're *actually* doing
- A habit of always changing your mind about what you want just when things are about to go "big" with what you've been working on (see section on Self-Sabotage in Chapter 2!)

If you've got big dreams that just never seem to go anywhere, then fear of success may very well be what's holding you back.

Bringing Your Fears into Your Conscious Mind

The best way to deal with these subconscious fears is to start becoming aware of them so that you can deal with them consciously. It starts with understanding that there are both good and bad aspects to any dream or goal that you have. So, if there is a particular goal that you've been working toward, ask yourself what would happen if you were successful.

Really take some time with it and think about it (this is not something that you do in thirty second – take at least 15 minutes to really think about what your life would be like if you were successful). Write down everything that comes to mind – the pros and the cons – and don't try to censor yourself; just let the ideas flow as they come.

The idea here is to let anything that might be hovering around just below surface level float to the top so you can actually see it. Oftentimes, just acknowledging any potential bad or scary stuff is enough to make it lose its grip on you.

Once you see the bad things for what they are and remember that they are just *possibilities* and not guaranteed fact, you can set up contingency plans to deal with them before they happen.

You can figure out ways to work around any potential bumps, you can do some research to find out how other people who have already achieved what you want to achieve deal with these same issues, or you can decide that the issues aren't as bad as they seem and that you're just going to live with them and be OK with them.

Facing your fear of success head-on and figuring out how you plan to deal with the inevitable changes that will come with your success before you get there is usually enough to get yourself back on track to achieving your original goal.

SUCCESS CAN'T CHANGE WHO YOU ARE

The other thing to keep in mind is that even though you may be afraid that you'll become someone you don't want to be — that you'll "forget where you came from" and become mean, arrogant, condescending, or otherwise unpleasant if you allow yourself to become successful – success in and of itself does not have the power to turn you into something you're not. A change in your circumstance cannot cause a change in your personality unless you allow it to. I think actor Will

Smith summed it up nicely when he said that "Money and success don't change people. They merely amplify what is already there."

An Example of Fear of Success

When I was just starting to branch into the new-to-me area of guest posting on other people's web sites, I was given a chance to really put my blog out there in front of a targeted audience of potentially tens of thousands of people who had never heard of me or VibeShifting.com before, and I really messed up.

I was supposed to write an article that was going to be reviewed, and possibly published, by a New York Times best-selling author in my field. And I could not, for the life of me, think of anything to write.

Moving Out of Your Comfort Zone

I had really pushed myself out of my comfort zone just by sending an email offering to write this person an article; my heart was pounding and my stomach was in knots just *thinking* about hitting the "send" button on that email. I was about to contact a *real, published, NYT best-selling author*, and I was seriously stressed over the audacity and sheer cheek of it all.

It was more daring than anything I'd ever done before, and I struggled with it for months before I was actually able to do it. And once it was done, I figured someone who was that cool would probably be super-busy and unlikely to check email all that often. I guessed that I probably had at least four weeks before I could expect a response, if I even got one at all.

Instead, I had a reply three days later that basically said "Sure, send one over. If I like it, I'll publish it." My stress level before sending the original email was nothing compared to what I felt on reading that response; I had thought that I would have at least a month to recover from my initial panic before I would even need to think about this!

CREATIVE BLOCK OR PROCRASTINATION?

So I kept putting it off and putting it off, even though I knew how *big* this opportunity was. And the question, of course, was *why*? Why, why, *why* would I be stalling on doing something with the potential to propel my biggest dream forward in a *huge* way?

It was a really good question. And it was something I asked myself over and over throughout the three months I struggled to come up with a topic idea (*any* topic idea!) for that article. Why couldn't I figure out what to write? What was holding me back? What the heck was going on?

WHAT IF I CAN'T HANDLE THE "NEXT LEVEL"?

I'm a writer, for heaven's sake – this is what I *do*. A simple 800 word essay in a topic area that I'm passionate about should have been child's play. But I could not get myself to sit down and write that article, no matter how many of my procrastination-busting strategies or creativity tricks I tried. And I could not for the life of me figure out what was stopping me from taking full advantage of this incredible opportunity to showcase my stuff.

And then I realized what it was that was holding me back: it was fear. I finally realized that this opportunity to reach that many people scared me, and that I was really intimidated by the thought of handing my work over to someone I consider famous (at least in the circles I work in).

What if this person didn't like my article? Or worse, what if the article got published and I suddenly got a huge influx of people all hitting my web site at once and my web host got mad at me? What if all those new people expected me to have programs and books and cool stuff like that when I didn't have any to offer them? What if they expected me to be some sort of big-shot expert and started asking me all sorts of questions that I didn't know the answers to and I ended up looking like a total idiot in front of an audience of tens of thousands?

I was worried that I couldn't put something together that was good enough to be seen at the "next level". I was afraid that *I* wasn't good enough for the next level.

THE TRICKIEST OF FEARS

Fear of success can be a tricky thing; it often camouflages itself as something else and can be very difficult to recognize because of it. And while my creative drought experience might, on the surface, seem like a classic case of fear of failure it was, in reality, less about being afraid to fail than it was about panicking over the thought of my work being seen by a potentially enormous audience. I wasn't sure that I was ready to deal with that, and my fears were causing a serious case of writer's block.

And so a golden opportunity nearly slipped out of my hands because I was too afraid to take the risk. It was self-sabotage of the highest order and in hindsight, it was absolutely ridiculous. But it happens, even to someone who blogs constantly about risks, dream-building, confidence, and taking action to create the kind of life you want.

Procrastination and fear of success are one of the most powerful dream-killing tag-teams out there, and even those of us who know how all this stuff works still get tripped up by them sometimes. If you have determined that procrastination is your main indicator of fear of success, then you absolutely must find ways to shake yourself out of the procrastination funk and get yourself moving again, quickly.

How to Stop Procrastinating

The next question, obviously, is: what do you do if inertia is already working against you and you're having problems getting started with taking any kind of action? There are lots of techniques out there that you can use to shake yourself into action-mode, but here are three of my personal favourites:

1. Use the "Ten Minute Rule"

The ten minute rule is a simple, yet handy technique to help you trigger yourself into action. It's a psychological trick for reducing the pressure and making the task seem less than it is. What you do is tell yourself you only have to do ten minutes of whatever the task is, and that's all you have to do. This often helps you to stop procrastinating by kicking that inertia thing into gear for you, and you find yourself doing the entire task or making major progress on it just because you got yourself started (whereas if you had gone into it thinking you'd have to do the whole thing, you just wouldn't have even begun).

For example, if you're trying to write a blog article but just can't seem to come up with anything, you reduce the pressure on yourself by telling yourself you only have to write for ten minutes – just a few sentences. And just by writing those few sentences, you often find yourself writing out the rest of the article anyway.

As another example, if you're trying to get yourself to hit the treadmill and get some exercise, you tell yourself that all you have to do is get your sweats and running shoes on, tie up your hair, and fill up your water bottle (because it will only take ten minutes), and by the time you've gotten your gear together, you usually find yourself following through and doing your half-hour run anyway.

2. CHANGE IT UP

Sometimes, you can shake yourself out of a procrastination funk just by changing the scenery or moving to a different environment. In some cases, all it takes to change it up is to change the layout or décor around your workspace – maybe move your desk to the other side of the room or change the posters on the wall or add an inspirational quote that will remind you to take action.

In other cases, packing up the laptop and heading to the local coffee shop to work can do wonders for helping you to stop procrastinating. Alternatively, the local library is one of my favourite places to regain my focus and motivation to get things done.

3. TAME THE TIME VAMPIRES

Time vampires show up when you have a certain list of things you plan to get done in a day, but then you get distracted by all the other random "to-do" items that always seem to crop up over the day, sucking your time away as you drop whatever you're doing to get those new items done at the expense of the original list. What happens then is that all of a sudden it's the end of the day and you realize that, while you've gotten a lot of those random, inconsequential tasks done you still haven't touched the original things you'd actually *planned* to do that day!

One of the methods I use to curb this problem is to use a daily agenda book (I just use an inexpensive academic planner that I bought at the local business supply store) to keep track of everything I want to do each day and each week. Those are the major tasks that I want to accomplish and the ones that I try and give priority to.

I also use a sticky note on the page to keep track of the random time vampires that pop up over the day. If the task that pops up isn't critical, I add it to the sticky note so I don't forget it, but I don't do it right away – I make sure to keep my focus on the main tasks and dedicate a specific amount of "vampire slaying time" at some point during the day to just blast through all of those extras all at once.

Sometimes, all it takes to get over that initial procrastination hurdle is one tiny step forward into action, so just pick something and start moving!

Dream, Believe, Achieve

The guiding principle behind everything that I teach through my blog, online courses, and personal coaching programs at VibeShifting.com is that "if you can dream it and believe it, you can *always* achieve it". This is because if you don't *believe* you can do something, you won't even try (and if you do believe, nothing will stop you).

But there's another part to this mantra, because it's not only about believing that you have the *ability* to do something, it's also about believing that you *deserve* to have it happen for you. If you don't believe that you deserve to live your dream — no matter how much you think you want it — it's not going to happen for you, because your subconscious is going to be sabotaging every attempt you make to get there and undermining your progress at every stage.

IMPOSTOR SYNDROME

This phenomenon of not believing that we deserve our success is often referred to as "Impostor Syndrome"[20]. It is very common (some estimates say that up to 70% of high-achieving individuals suffer from it), and it is one of the biggest dream-killers out there.

Basically, those who suffer from Impostor Syndrome chalk their successes up to luck or fluke and they are terrified that they cannot live up to the image that they believe other people have of them.

Oftentimes, these people are also perfectionists who secretly believe that they are frauds for having achieved the things they have when their own lives are not the shining examples of perfection that they believe the lives of successful people *should* be. Those with Imposter Syndrome do not believe that they deserve their own success.

THERE'S NOTHING YOU HAVE TO PROVE

This syndrome is one of the saddest aspects of fear of success, because the truth of the matter is that just the fact that we want what we want is enough.

From a cosmic perspective, there's nothing we have to prove, no penance we have to pay, no sacrifices we have to make in order to be deserving of what it is that we want.

We are deserving of our dreams by virtue of our existence alone; we were *born* deserving of them.

It's only through the fears, negativity, and judgment that we have picked up from the outside that we come to doubt our deserving-ness. But these internalized fears are often so ingrained that we don't even realize that we have them; we keep sabotaging ourselves by not doing what we know we need to do to get to where we want to be, and we don't even realize that we're doing it because, deep inside, we don't believe we deserve to have our dreams come true.

BELIEVING YOU DESERVE YOUR DREAMS

If this belief that we don't deserve our success is such a deeply hidden thing, then how can we even tell it's something we're dealing with? Here's the test: Focus on your big dream, get really clear in your mind about what it is and what it would mean. And then say out loud "I deserve to have this." And pay very close attention to how you *feel* when you say it.

Is there excitement? Joy? A sense of anticipation? Or is there more of a sense of dread, discomfort, sadness or shame? Does your stomach tighten up or feel "off" when you say it?

The way you *feel* when you tell yourself that you deserve your dream will immediately tell you what you *really* believe. And if anything feels the least bit off, then you know you have some serious mindset-shifting work to do. Because if your stomach is telling you that you don't believe you deserve to have your dream come true, then you know that your *expectations* are not aligned with it. And it is your expectations that determine your reality.

Making the Mental Shift

So how do you make that shift and start convincing yourself that you really do deserve to be successful? Here is a five-step process to help:

Step 1: Write It Down

If you haven't yet taken the time to do your first action exercise from chapter 1 yet, do it now: write your dream down. Write out in detail what your dream is, what it would mean to you to have it come true. Really get yourself connected to the dream.

Step 2: Why Don't You Deserve It?

If you already know that you don't think you deserve to have your dream or if you're in that fuzzy "I think I deserve it, but..." state of mind, then write down all those reasons and all those "buts". They could include things like:

- Yes, I can help people, but I'm not an expert! People are going to find out I'm a fake.
- I'm good at it, but other people are so much better than I am.
- My family thinks this is a stupid waste of time.
- I'm just being selfish.
- No one else I know has a life like that. Why should I be any different?
- I'm not pretty enough/ smart enough/ dedicated enough/ whatever enough.
- I've failed at everything else I've ever tried.

Write down every reason, every "but" that comes to mind, and don't take the time at this point to analyse or rationalize any of them – just get them all out and written down on paper and keep writing until nothing else comes out.

STEP 3: THE OBJECTIVE RESPONSE

Now it's time to take that rational, objective look at each of your items and come up with responses to them. For each one of your reasons and "buts", I want you to write down *why it isn't true* because *none* of these answers are real; they're just gremlins coming out of the woodwork to bring you down. They're shadows, nothing more; straw men with no substance, and it's time for you to tear them down.

So, for example, if you feel that you've failed at everything before, I want you to think back and remember a time when you *did* succeed at something you tried. Write that memory down. For instance: "Well, there was that time when I wanted to build a picnic table from scratch. Everyone thought it was a dumb idea because they're so easy to buy pre-made. But I wanted a bigger one and I really wanted to see if I could make it myself, and I did! I even custom-sized it to fit our big family, and I painted it blue, my mom's favourite colour. She loved it – in fact, she still uses it every summer for our family picnic!"

STEP 4: MIRROR WORK

This is the tough part. Find yourself a mirror and some quiet time where you know you won't be interrupted. Look yourself in the eye and tell yourself, out loud, that you deserve to have this dream come true. (Fair warning — there could be tears and there could be anger. Let it happen. Let it out.)

Spend three minutes with this exercise and then stop for the day. But do it again for three minutes once or twice a week until you no longer have any negative reaction to it. Keep doing it until you start to believe that it's true.

Step 5: Use Your Affirmations

Only do the mirror exercise a couple of times per week, and only for a few minutes at a time (it's powerful and can be emotionally draining), but supplement the mirror work with the use of daily affirmations. For example:

- I deserve to find the perfect job.
- I deserve to be a successful entrepreneur.
- I deserve to be accepted into this graduate program.
- I deserve to be in a loving, fulfilling relationship.

If affirmations that strong don't feel right to you (if they are too much of a stretch to be believable to you), then try something softer, such as "I am willing to learn that I deserve _____" or "I am becoming more comfortable with my own deserving-ness." Whatever your dream is, create a personalized affirmation to help you understand how much you deserve to be living that dream. And repeat that affirmation to yourself frequently throughout the day.

Belief is a powerful thing, and belief in yourself is even more so. This process will help you break down any old, ingrained programming that's affecting your beliefs about whether or not you deserve to have your dreams become a reality. It will help to clear all that old junk out of your head and pave the way for really aligning yourself with what you want.

Chapter 6 Recap

❖ **Key Points to Remember:**

- Fear of success is rarely conscious. Most people who struggle with it don't realize that they do.
- Your subconscious fears about the negative implications of potential success are preventing you from achieving what you want to.
- Procrastination is one of biggest signs of a fear of success.
- People with Impostor Syndrome tend to believe that they are frauds who don't deserve their success.

❖ **Your Action Items:**

1. Complete the exercise on page 102 to uncover your hidden fears about the negative aspects of your success.
2. Review the exercises for overcoming procrastination on page 107 and be sure to use them next time you are procrastinating.
3. Focus completely on your big dream then say out loud: "I deserve to have this." Make note of what you feel when you say it. If it feels anything but awesome, be sure to do action item #4, below.
4. Complete the 5 step process on page 112 to start shifting your mindset into believing you deserve your own success.

❖ **Download:**

- http://www.VibeShifting.com/fearless-bonus

Chapter 7:
The Fear of Judgement

PEOPLE WILL LOVE YOU. PEOPLE WILL HATE YOU.
AND NONE OF IT WILL HAVE ANYTHING TO DO WITH YOU.
~Esther Hicks, American Author and Inspirational Speaker

There are so many people in this world who hold themselves back from really going after the things they most want to achieve because they are afraid of what people will think; they are afraid that others will laugh at their dreams or think those dreams are ridiculous ("Who do you think you are?" or "You want to do *what? Seriously?*")

When it comes to the fear of judgement, there are two aspects that we have to take into consideration: the judgement we feel from the outside world, and the internal judgement that we subject ourselves to. It's hard enough trying to build a dream without having to listen to all the haters, both inside and outside of you, tell you that you're deluded, stupid, crazy, materialistic or otherwise just not good enough to make it happen. So in this chapter we're going to look at ways of recognizing and coping with all of that nastiness so that it can't hold you back anymore.

Your Dreams Are Never "Wrong"

One of the recurring themes in the emails I get from my readers is this idea that we shouldn't want what we want in life because it's "selfish" – because it's too much or too big or too lavish or just too different from what other people in our lives want, and because those other people disapprove of that. On the flip side, some people have very simple dreams in their hearts, and it is the fact that their dreams aren't lofty *enough*, according to the standards of those around them, that triggers the outside disapproval.

For the love of All That Is, I am *begging* you to get all of that garbage out of your head! And let me make this very, very clear:

You're allowed to want what you want!

It doesn't matter if what you want is to have a 50 000 square-foot house with gold bathtubs and diamond windows. It doesn't matter if you want to live in a one-room cabin and run a non-profit organic farming commune. It doesn't matter if you want to do nothing all day except golf. It doesn't matter if you want to sell everything you own, move into a cave on a mountaintop in Peru and spend the rest of your life in silent meditation while ignoring the rest of world. It doesn't matter if you want fame, fortune, and your face on the cover every magazine out there. It doesn't matter if you want to be a stay-at-home mother with 5 kids, a white picket fence and a hamster. And it doesn't matter if you want to do *all* of the above at one point or another in your lifetime. You are allowed to want whatever it is that you want!

Deciding that any of the above (or any other dream for that matter) is wrong is a completely subjective judgement call. Why should we try to decide what constitutes an acceptable dream for another person? As long as we aren't hurting ourselves or anyone else, and as long as we find joy in what we are doing, then what does it matter if we want something that other people in our lives would never in a million years choose for themselves, or vice-versa? What a dull and boring world it would be if we all wanted do, have, and be the same things!

No one has the right to tell you that you can't want what you want. If you want to live a life of austerity and renounce all material possessions, go for it. But if you want to be rich and famous, then you have every right to want that for yourself, too – and there is nothing wrong with that.

Gratitude is the Foundation for Your Dreams

The idea that wanting more in life is somehow wrong is a direct result of thinking that where we are and what we have right now is not enough. And that *is* a problem, because appreciating all that we have at whatever stage we are currently at is really important.

There is absolutely nothing wrong with wanting more (of whatever) in your life, but the way to get more (of anything) is to wholeheartedly appreciate what already exists. When we believe that we do not have enough – that we are lacking in some way – then we are setting ourselves up for a lifetime of lack. Oprah Winfrey said it best when she said: "Be thankful for what you have; you'll end up having more. If you concentrate on what you don't have, you will never, ever have enough."

Gratitude really is the foundation upon which you build your extraordinary life, so appreciate everything that you already have, no matter how small or insignificant you think it is. What we are focused on is what we tend to bring more of into our lives, so if we get stuck in a mindset that says "I don't have enough", then we will never feel like we have enough, no matter how much we have.

If we can shift our perspective to one of appreciation, however, then we will consistently find more in our lives to be appreciative of. But it has to be genuine; fake gratitude just for the sake of trying to *get* something else isn't going to work, because you're not truly grateful in that case – you're still focused on lack. So just focus on being honestly grateful for whatever wonderful things already exist in your life, even if it's as small as a sunny day or an unexpected smile from the girl at the coffee shop drive-through window.

This does not, in any way, mean that you can't or shouldn't have greater abundance in your life; by all means work on that and get excited about the possibilities! Dream big and want whatever it is that you want; you're allowed to and you are *meant* to. But never allow those dreams to make you complacent or indifferent to what you already have; don't take anything for granted. Be happy with where you are while you work to create where you want to be.

I'll Never Be Good Enough (Coping with Your Inner Critic)

So many of us look toward our idols - the ones who are already doing what we want to do - with a mixture of excitement, envy, and sadness because we wish so desperately that we could just be where they are. We want so much to just be able to figure out that magic key that will get us to where we want to be, right now. But the problem is that, at our core, we don't really *believe* that it is possible for us to ever get there. We don't really believe that we could ever be what we most want to be, because we're not sure we really deserve it and because we're not sure that we're good enough to accomplish it.

The thing you need to understand about this is that all those voices you hear inside your head, telling you that you'll never make it, that you're not good enough, that you still have to do more before you'll be worthy; all those voices that compare you to everyone else - you *must* stop listening to them. Because nothing you do will *ever* satisfy them.

You could have achieved every goal you've ever had, earned every accolade available and won every prize that's out there, and those voices would still tell you that you're not good enough. But it's not true; what those voices say is all just smoke and mirrors designed to make you fear your own dreams.

Getting to Know Your Gremlins

In Chapter 4 we talked about the difference between primary and secondary fears and discovered that a lot of the fears that you've been holding onto all your life were never really yours to begin with; rather, they are fears that you have picked up through your associations with other people (usually your family members or close connections).

This is a really important point to be aware of because the one thing you really need to understand about the nasty, judgmental voices inside your own head is that they were never yours. We are not born with an inner critic; we are infected with one. The voices of wisdom, guidance, and conscience *are* meant to be there, but not outright negativity and nastiness; those are voices and opinions that we have picked up from the outside world.

I like to refer to the nastiest of these negative inner voices as "gremlins", those spiteful little voices inside of us that make us doubt ourselves and worry about all the things that *could* go wrong when things are, in fact, going right.

Gremlins delight in pointing out the obvious every time we screw up. They are a particularly nasty kind of inner critic because they feed on fear, which triggers that primitive "fight or flight" response within us, which in turn tends to circumvent our ability to calmly and rationally think our way through a situation, or to work our way through to a better feeling place; all of which means that these gremlins have the power to completely undermine our efforts to make progress towards our biggest dreams and goals.

What Gremlins Do

Gremlins are incredibly stubborn and persistent, which makes them all the worse. They're kind of like that "Whack-A-Mole" game at the fair — whenever you start making progress towards something that is important to you, the little gremlins pop their heads up out of nowhere and start spewing negativity at you. They will come up with every conceivable reason why you can't have what you want, and if you let yourself listen to what they're saying, it can really start to undermine your self-confidence and your ability to keep taking those action steps you need to take in order to reach your goals.

Gremlins have a vested interest in keeping you from achieving your goals because if you're successful, their very existence is threatened. At the same time, however, gremlins don't want you to completely give up on your goals, either. They desperately need you to keep working towards that dream *up to a point*; they want you to *strive*, but they don't want you to *succeed*, because they feed on your fear, and they feed on your frustration. And if you either achieve your goals or give up on them, then they don't get fed.

So they're unlikely to kill your dreams completely; they would much rather keep you in that horrible limbo, carefully balanced on a wire where you can keep generating the maximum amount of both fear and frustration to keep them fat and happy. Remember what I said about the "Whack-A-Mole" game? They pop their heads up until they get a satisfying reaction from you, and then they disappear again until the next time you start to get too close to making real things happen.

INNER CRITIC OR INNER WISDOM?

When I've talked about gremlins in the past, I've had people ask me how they're supposed to tell if that voice they're hearing is their Inner Critic or their Inner Wisdom. How do you distinguish between gremlins and what I usually refer to as "the whisper within" – your inner guidance or inner wisdom – trying to tell you that this is really not the best path for you to take?

Well, that takes a little bit of patience. It involves taking the time to be still and really look within for the answers. Check in with your emotions; when you think about what you're trying to do, are you afraid, but still excited about it, or are you afraid and dreading it right to the pit of your stomach?

If there's fear, but still excitement, it's probably the right path for you and working through the fear is the best step you can take to bring yourself closer to your dream. If there's mostly terror or a sickening sense of dread, then listen to that and don't do it – it's probably not the best path, or just not the right time.

DOING IT ANYWAY

If you're pretty sure that what you're dealing with is a gremlin rather than a serious inner warning, then the best thing to do is to continue what you're doing. Acknowledge the fear, but keep moving towards your goal anyway.

Shift your focus back to what you're working towards, take some time to remember your *why*; reconnect with your touchstones and all the reasons you had for working towards this dream in the first place. (We'll talk more about the importance of your big "*why*" in Chapter 10!)

Remember that you deserve to have your dream come true – there's nothing you need to prove to anyone else, and no dues you have to pay in order to "earn" the privilege of having your dreams become a reality. Your dreams are in your heart for a reason, and the fact that they are even there at all is all the proof in the world that they are meant to come true. Reconnect with all of that, and then pull on your "determination boots" and keep going.

Eventually those gremlins will get the picture and give you some peace. They are unlikely to ever disappear completely (they are tenacious little beasties) but after a while, they won't be so loud anymore.

How to Tame Your Gremlins

"Well, that's just great", you're saying, "but *how*, exactly am I supposed to just keep going when I've got gremlins shouting at me?" The best way to banish gremlins is to change the way you look at them. Remember that what we resist persists; if we're focused on *fighting* the gremlins that just makes them stronger. So what we do is use gentler strategies to work around them, instead:

Strategy #1: Imagine it's a Pet

Go back to the "Whack-A-Mole" game. Annoying though it is to have bad-tempered gremlins popping their heads up just when you least want to deal with them, they could be kind of cute if you looked at them a little differently.

Imagine the gremlin as a cranky, but adorable cartoon character or a really yappy little dog. Yeah, it can get irritating at times, but you do tend to grow fond of it after a while and might even miss it if it weren't around. So when one of those gremlins pops its head up, imagine yourself patting it on the top of its ugly little head; tell it to "shush" and then toss it a stick or something to keep it occupied while you get back to work.

Strategy #2: Imagine it's Your Highly Opinionated Granny

When your gremlin pops its head up, imagine it's someone's cantankerous, slightly senile, but dearly loved old granny.

Imagine yourself having tea with her and picture her grouching at you over her knitting as she sits in her rocking chair (I have little kids, so I like to imagine her as Granny Smith from the *My Little Pony* cartoons, but feel free to use whatever image works for you).

You're there to have tea and don't want to get into a discussion about your life plans because you know where you're going and how to get there, but Granny's got her own ideas and insists on telling you that you're doing things wrong, you're making a mistake, such things simply weren't done back in her day, or whatever.

She just won't stop nattering and she's driving you crazy with her unsolicited advice, but you really do love her and you don't want to hurt her feelings. So you just sip your tea, smile, and nod like you're listening, all the while knowing that at some point she will get tired of talking and fall asleep.

STRATEGY #3: MAKE IT LAUGH

One of my blog readers said that she likes to imagine herself giving her gremlin a hug, thanking it for its input, and then tickling its belly until it giggles. I thought that was priceless – that would definitely throw a gremlin off-stride and send it scurrying away in confusion!

Basically, if you can shift your perspective with regards to your gremlins – when you can find a way to laugh at them or to love them – then they lose their power over you. You don't need to fight them or destroy them, you just need to change the way you think about them.

. . . . .

Sticks and Stones
(Coping With Outside Critics)

"Sticks and stones may break my bones but words will never hurt me". It's a rhyme many of us were taught as small children as a way to cope with being teased and called names by other children. We all used it, but we all knew just how hollow it really was.

The truth, of course, is that words *do* hurt. And they can cause wounds that last longer than any mere physical injury. Words can do a real number on you, especially when you internalize them and start spewing the same sort of negativity at *yourself*. There is a cumulative effect to negativity and as you will learn in Chapter 9, seemingly minor, negative thought habits can actually poison your entire outlook on life. Words are powerful, and they have the ability to change the course of your entire life... if you let them.

When you've spent a lifetime listening to other people tell you that you're not good enough or that there's something wrong with you for thinking the way that you do or for wanting the kind of life you want, it can be really hard to push through all of that and still get yourself to where you want to be. But it is possible. And if your dream means enough to you, you will have to find a way to do it. That doesn't mean that you will never feel hurt by those outside voices – you will. It doesn't mean that there will never be tears or anger over their words – there will be. It just means that, rather than trapping those feelings inside of you and letting them fester, you will let them flow through you and then you will pick yourself up, dry your tears, and keep going.

Haters Gonna Hate

One of the most important skills you will ever learn is how to keep yourself from being overly affected by the negative views and criticism of other people. There is a quote floating around the internet that is widely, though falsely, attributed to the ancient Greek philosopher Aristotle (in actuality, the quote was most likely adapted from something said by 19th Century American writer Elbert Hubbard), and it says that the only way to avoid criticism is to do nothing, say nothing, and be nothing.

In other words, if you don't want anyone to say anything mean to you in life, then don't do anything that could ever possibly attract attention.

If you had no goals in life, that might actually work. But when you have a big dream that you're trying to build, you're going to start making waves and attracting attention from the outside world, and any time that happens, you will attract critics. Like moths to a flame – if you're going to shine, people will be drawn to that light. Some of them will be supportive, and some of them will just try to tear you down. You are going to have to be strong enough to shake any negativity off; strong enough to remember who you are; and strong enough to remember why your dream is more important than whatever anyone else will throw at you. Haters will always hate, but you can choose not to listen to them.

Why We Let Their Opinions Matter

Human beings are hardwired to fear being shunned by or excluded from whatever group we feel we belong to. Back in the caveman days, a lone individual had very little chance of survival without the protection of the larger group, and being exiled was tantamount to a death sentence.

In order to improve our odds of survival, we therefore evolved a sensitive mechanism to help us detect the kinds of social currents that might indicate that we were about to be kicked out of the group, along with an internal fail-safe system that pressured us to do whatever it took to conform to the dictates of the group and retain our membership therein.

This is why it still hurts so much today when we feel that we are being ostracized by others, and why we still try so hard to fit into our perceived social groups.[21] It's one of the main reasons why it bothers us so much when people say mean things to us.

Complicating this is the fact that, because human beings are completely helpless at birth, we are also hardwired to put a lot of value into the opinions and beliefs of those who raise us. We have to because they're the ones who keep us alive. This often translates into an unconscious belief that the opinion of *anyone* in a position of authority (and that can be interpreted as anyone with more confidence that we have) should be given greater consideration than our own.

Unfortunately, all this primitive conditioning that we're born with can have very detrimental effects once we are old enough to start making our own decisions and living our own lives. Often, if our own internal wisdom is at odds with what we've been taught, either directly or indirectly, we feel that there must be something wrong with *ourselves* for thinking the way we do. And so we squash those whispers inside of us that tell us what we're really meant to do here.

Why Their Words Hurt So Much

You already intuitively know to love yourself; it's the reason it feels so awful when people say horrible things to you. You can *feel* that it is an untruth because the real you knows how wonderful you are. You are light. You are love. You are infinite Source. When people say mean things designed to hurt you, and when they tell you that what you want most in life isn't acceptable, it *does* hurt because it clashes so strongly with the truth inside of you; there is a fundamental discord happening within you.

Remember that you come from a place of unconditional love; this is who you really are. And you have a gift within you that you came here to give. That gift also came from that place of unconditional love, and it is a gift that only you can give. Because it is so unique to you, when you are told that it isn't good enough, or that it will never happen, it affects you to your core. Your very purpose seems undermined or devalued somehow.

It's How You Choose to React

But remember that it is not what happens to us, or what other people say to us, that matters most. It is how we choose to *react* to those situations that matters. We do have a *choice* about how we let the words and opinions of other people affect us.

I'm not going to brush it off and tell you it's easy to just let that kind of stuff slide off of you. This kind of conditioning goes deep; it is rooted in our most basic survival instincts, after all. But it is just a form of programming – just another set of thought habits. And habits can always be changed.

Once you know what is actually happening in these situations, you can start taking conscious steps to try and counteract the effects. You can choose to recognize that the calling within your own soul is more important than any outside opinion could ever be. You can choose to be stronger than whatever is trying to hurt you.

Pain Only Comes From Pain

Something else to keep in mind is that when people try to hurt you, in any way, it is because they are in some sort of pain themselves; pain only ever comes from pain. In most cases, when people bash your dreams, it's because they have already given up on their own and that hurts a lot, and on a very deep level. And that kind of pain tends to show itself in the form of trying to stop other people from realizing their own dreams in a "misery loves company" kind of way.

But you are the only one who can decide whether to continue working towards a particular dream or not; this is *your* life and *you* get to choose your path. If you decide you are going to continue following your dream, then you have to be strong enough to ignore the sticks and stones and hurtful words of those around you. Channel those feelings into building the foundation for something phenomenal.

Shifting Your Perspective

One of the best techniques for coping with outside criticism is to just change your attitude about it. The most important thing to do is to realize that when these others are attacking you for something wonderful that you've achieved, or are in the process of achieving, it's actually a *good* sign; it means that you're on track and making progress! If you've made enough changes that people are getting angry about it, it's an indication that whatever you're doing is working (congratulations!) Just this one attitude shift alone can go a long way to making it easier for you to deal with the "Negative Nellies" that surround you.

Whenever you get dumped on, remind yourself that this is proof that you're accomplishing your goals, and let it slide off you like you're Teflon®. Have fun with it, even! Set up a chart, and every time someone says something mean, add another tick to your tally of proof that you're getting somewhere, and get excited about it: "Woo-hoo! Another pot shot from the critics – I must really be *crushing* this thing now!"

It's so easy to tear other people down, but it takes a special kind of courage to put yourself out there in front of the crowd and build something extraordinary. It takes ingenuity, heart and a great deal of strength. Always remember that those who are busy knocking others down rarely take the time to build anything of consequence themselves. Take heart, and stay focused on your dreams.

What if The Critics Are Family?

Some of the most stressful situations we find ourselves in, in terms of outside criticism, tend to revolve around our relationships with family. No one seems to be able to push our buttons like our family members can. These are the people for whom most of us have been conditioned to show unquestioning loyalty towards. So, when they hurt us, we really tend to feel that pain particularly deeply. We take it very personally, and there is a lot of resentment and feelings of betrayal in there, too.

When you get to that time and place in your life when you start taking real steps towards creating the kind of life that YOU really want, rather than just living your life according to the wishes and expectations of your family, and this can happen at any age, by the way – some people hit that stage when they are teenagers, and some of us don't get there until much later in life – but when you do get to that stage and start running your life and making decisions from the perspective of what's best for *you*, then that tends to get the family up in arms. Especially if you've always been the kind of person to listen to the advice and direction of your family, and have always done what you're told.

When you start making changes in your life, either through your actions or your ways of thinking, it causes ripple effects that spread outward and touch everyone you know. When you make a big change, it forces other people to change as well; they now have to completely revise how they interact with you and how they think about you. And that's really uncomfortable. You used to be predictable, and now, all of a sudden, you're not (how dare you!).

It's Not About You, It's About Them

Their reactions, however, really have nothing to do with you, what you're achieving or what you're becoming. Their reactions have everything to do with their own desperate attempts to cling to the familiar. Human beings are prone to something called "negativity bias", wherein we focus more on the bad things that happen and ignore the good because the bad things could be dangerous and therefore require more attention.

And this negativity bias really comes into play when someone who is a part of your life starts to change – it's often interpreted as a danger signal because people, as we'll learn in the next chapter, tend to fear the unknown. It goes something like this: "You're becoming different; I don't know or understand what that's going to entail; it scares the crap out of me, and I want you to stop it right now because it's making *me* uncomfortable!"

THE COCONUT FARM EXPERIMENT

One of the things that makes family-generated criticism all the harder for people to deal with is how complete strangers are often so much more supportive of their dreams and goals than the people they care about the most. Why is that? Why are strangers more supportive than family when it comes to all this stuff?

Let's just do a little thought experiment here, and imagine what would happen if you told your family that you wanted to quit your job, move to Fiji, and set up a cooperative, fair-trade coconut farm and yoga retreat.

Unless you happen to have an unusually supportive family, they'd probably look at you like you'd gone *coconuts*, and tell you you're being completely ridiculous and that you can't possibly move to Fiji. They'd come up with every possible reason why it could never happen, and they'd insist that you stop being so flighty and be reasonable. And then they'd probably say something along the lines of: "doesn't Aunt Marjory know a man at the Acme Widget Corporation downtown who might be able to get you a nice, respectable job as a clerk?"

And all of a sudden, your big dream is shot down and labelled "IMPOSSIBLE", before you've even gotten started.

ENTHUSIASTIC STRANGERS

If, however, you decided to strike up a conversation with a couple of complete strangers at a coffee shop, for instance, and you told them your Fiji coconut dream, it would most likely spark their imaginations. They'd be far more likely to start brainstorming ways of making it happen.

Maybe one of them has a brother who has a buddy whose sister spent a year in Fiji and still has a few contacts there who could scout out a great location for a yoga retreat. And maybe the other one works for a health food store that needs a new source for organic coconut oil products and could put you in touch with their corporate buyer.

And the really hot guy at the other table who was listening in on your conversation turns around and says that he actually runs a yoga studio in town, but he's been dreaming of running a tropical yoga retreat for years, and would you perhaps like to swap ideas over dinner? And all of a sudden, your big dream doesn't look so impossible anymore.

Now, I said this was a thought experiment, but I'm going to give you a challenge: Go out there and actually give this experiment a try! Think of something completely outrageous (you could even use this coconut farm example if you want), and tell some stranger in a coffee shop or a bar or a library that this is your big dream, but you're not sure the best way get started, or that you don't have any contacts in this field or part of the world, or whatever. And just see what happens.

Just give it a try and see how many ideas a complete stranger generates to try and make that outrageous dream a reality. (And please note that I make no guarantees that you're going to get a dinner date out of this experiment, but you never know...)

WHY ARE STRANGERS MORE SUPPORTIVE THAN FAMILY?

So, why is this? Why does this happen? Why would complete strangers who have no idea who you are be so much more likely to help you find ways to make even your craziest dreams a reality? And why would your family – the people whom, you'd think, should be the ones most likely to be in your corner, be so quick to shoot your dreams down?

In large part, it comes down to the fact that they had dreams of their own that they gave up on. And their efforts to prevent you from reaching your own dreams come from fear and pain; the fear that you'll get hurt, and the pain of seeing someone else doing or achieving something when they had to give their own dreams up, and when they no longer believe those dreams are even remotely possible anymore.

THEY'RE TRYING TO PROTECT YOU

So let's take a closer look at these reasons. And the first one we said was that your family may be afraid for you, and they may be trying to protect you. This is often the biggest reason behind the criticism in situations where your parents are particularly negative with regards to your dreams. Because remember that they all started out with hopes and dreams, once, just like you did. But many of them started families shortly after they left their own parent's homes to begin venturing forth and living their own lives. So their dreams were dashed early on as they had to cope with the realities of having children and mortgages and big responsibilities.

And it cost them big-time; when people give up on their dreams it hurts an awful lot. And perhaps, in seeing you reaching for *your* dreams, your parents are actually afraid for you; afraid that you may also end up having to give up those dreams of yours and that you, like them, will then end up having to feel that same pain. A lot of this dream-bashing, then, comes from your family's *fear* for you; they love you and don't want to see you get hurt.

BITTERNESS AND REGRET

The other thing that sometimes happens when people give up on their own dreams and stop believing in the possibility of them ever coming true is that there's bitterness and a jadedness that goes along with that. When you give up on what your heart wants most and then try to convince yourself that you're better off without it anyway it changes you, in fundamental ways.

We're all born with that bit of magic in us, that unique gift that each and every one of has – the one that we came here to share with the world – and when we deny that gift, smother it, or otherwise fail to bring it into the light of day, we suffer for it. And people in that kind of pain will instinctively lash out at anyone who hasn't let their own dream die because it hurts too much to see that bit of magic in someone else when you think that yours is gone for good.

Except that it's never completely gone. Dreams don't die. They can't; they're too much a part of us. Reconnecting with them is just a matter of listening to that little whisper within once again. It's never too late to create your dream.

Just keep moving towards it in whatever way you can, and keep yourself aligned with that vision while you work towards it. And it will always be enough.

But if you can't see that, if you don't *believe* that it's possible for you anymore, then seeing other people who still have that hope and that drive to build their own dreams is just too painful.

And that's where a lot of the dream-bashing from our families comes from. And just to note here: I've been talking about parents, but, because your siblings have been brought up in much the same environment that you have, they would have picked up these same sorts of attitudes, perspectives, and beliefs from your parents. So if you're in a situation where your brothers or sisters are giving you a hard time, then this really all comes from the same place. It's all the same source.

Strategies for Coping with Family Critics

So what do you do about it? How do you deal with the family bashing your biggest dreams? When people get frightened like this, getting backed into that corner of having to deal with your changes head-on, then can get pretty vocal about their disapproval. They can even get down-right nasty sometimes, which can cause you to start questioning your own decisions and the wisdom of your new path in life.

But there are a few things that you can do to keep yourself on track with your own dreams and goals, despite whatever verbal assaults others may throw at you:

AVOID THE "HOT-BUTTONS"

My usual recommendation for dealing with this type of situation is that you just don't talk about your dreams with your family. If discussion of all the things that you're trying to build in your life just creates tension and stress for you, then don't go there; save your dream-building discussions for your friends or your networking group. And if you don't already have that support system, then you need to build that kind tribe for yourself (or come and join the Vibe Shifters Tribe[22], my free discussion group on Facebook!)

BUFFER YOURSELF

If you do happen to get sucked into one of those horrible dream-killing conversations, learn to build a buffer around yourself. If you can't excuse yourself from the discussion, just nod politely and smile while the other person talks at you, thank them for their input, tell them they've given you much to think about, and then walk away and put the entire conversation out of your mind. And then go and do your thing anyway. Your life is YOUR life and yours alone. And you are the only one who gets to call the shots.

STAY CALM

When people start in on you about your dreams and goals, resist the temptation to fight fire with fire, no matter how nasty they get. Remember that much of what these people are throwing at you is born of their own fear; fear that either *they* will have to change, too, in order to fit in with the "new you" or fear that they may no longer fit with you at all and will end up losing you.

These are legitimate fears, and if you can keep that in mind in the face of their personal attacks, then it becomes easier to understand without being bothered by it. And what often happens is that because you remain so calm and demonstrate that you're willing to listen to them, the other people feel more secure. Their fears then start to evaporate and they stop badgering you to change back to the way you were.

REMEMBER YOUR TRUTH

If the person you're dealing with is calm enough, try stating your own position and thoughts clearly and calmly. "I am choosing a healthier lifestyle because I value myself as a person and believe that I am worth the effort" or "I am changing my major because I love this subject and feel most alive when I am doing something that I believe in", or whatever.

The other person may not care one bit about what you've said, but it will help *you* to hear yourself state, out loud, why you're doing what you're doing and why you've chosen the path you have. It's a powerful reminder from your inner voice that will help you to stay on track despite what happens outside. If you're not feeling strong enough to voice this to the other person, that's OK; wait until you're alone and try it as mirror work: look into your own eyes and tell *yourself* why you're doing this.

WEATHERING THE STORMS

When you start making changes in your life and commit yourself to building your dream it's exciting and scary all at once. You're proud of your accomplishments and a little overwhelmed by all that's happening. Having to deal the stress of close family's disapproval on top of all of this can really take a toll on your self-esteem and ability to keep making the changes you want to see in your life. But understanding that this outside hostility is a smokescreen for fear, remaining calm in the face of resentment, and remembering the reason why you're making the changes you are will help you to stay focused and weather the family-related storms.

BIG DREAMS INSPIRE EVERYONE

The other thing to remember is that people will bash your dreams until they start to happen for you. At which point they will start to wonder how you did it, and may just magically turn into your biggest supporters!

Big dreams have a tendency to inspire everyone they touch. So don't worry too much if your family doesn't support you right now; find your support in other places, and keep building your dreams. Eventually your family will come around, and maybe they'll be so motivated by all that you've achieved that they'll start finding ways to make their own dreams happen. And then they'll all be happier people for it.

Chapter 7 Recap

- ❖ *Key Points to Remember:*
    - There are two aspects to the fear of judgement: internal judgement, which comes from our own inner critics, and outer judgment, which comes from other people.
    - It doesn't matter what your dream is or how different it is from everyone else's; you're allowed to want what you want!
    - Gremlins are a particularly nasty form of inner critic that you will have to deal with.
    - Our reactions to outside criticism are often rooted in our most basic survival instincts; this is why it hurts so much. Shifting the way you look at this criticism will help you to cope with it (and even have fun with it!)
    - Family members are often the biggest dream-bashers out there. This is often done out of their own fears for you.

- ❖ *Your Action Items:*
    1. Review the strategies for taming gremlins on page 125.
    2. Create your "Critic Pot-Shots" tally chart and start tracking your "proof of progress".
    3. Try the Coconut Farm Experiment on page 134.
    4. Review the strategies for coping with family-based critics on page 138.

- ❖ *Download:*
    - http://www.VibeShifting.com/fearless-bonus

Chapter 8: The Fear of the Unknown

> You don't need to see the whole staircase.
> Just take the first step in faith.
> ~ Martin Luther King Jr., American Civil Rights Activist

For many of us, the fear of not being able to see exactly how the goal will be achieved at every turn is terrifying, and being unable to see the whole path all at once prevents us from ever taking the first step. But what if that first step is all it takes to break through that psychological barrier? What if the very act of committing to our goal and taking that first step in the faith that we can and will be successful is enough to evaporate our fear?

Out of all of the fears we've looked at so far, fear of the unknown is by far the biggest and most prevalent and in fact, all of the other fears are based, in some way, on this one fear. Everything comes down to the fear of not knowing what's going to happen next. When we can't see the whole route, when we don't know exactly what's going to happen and when, it stresses us out. We are afraid of what *could* happen, and this is what fear *really* is – the product of our own overactive imaginations creating monsters in the dark that were never there to begin with. And when you think about it that way, letting our fears control the direction and outcome of our lives really doesn't make much sense at all, does it?

When you're driving through the fog, you can't see more than ten feet in front of you, but that doesn't mean that there is no road. It appears out of the fog, as if by magic, as you inch yourself forward through the unknown. You can choose to sit and stubbornly refuse to move at all until the fog disappears (except that, unlike meteorological fog, the fog from the unknown elements in your life is never going to clear up completely), or you can take a risk, carefully start moving forward, and maybe end up somewhere incredible.

You Will Never Have All the Answers

So often we put off getting started on our dreams because we have no idea how we're going to make them happen. We don't want to take that first step until we know exactly how we're going to get from Point A to Point B, and we're not prepared to take a risk on doing something that might fail until we're sure that it won't. There are so many questions along that unknown path, and we're just not prepared to start moving until we get some guarantees; until we get our answers.

But you're never going to have all the answers; it just doesn't happen that way. The answers, like the questions themselves, change as the path forms – as you *create* your path. You can't have all the answers to something that hasn't happened yet. And much as you'd like to, you can't see the whole path laid out before you, because it doesn't exist yet. You're the one who builds it as you go. And really... where's the adventure in knowing everything that's going to happen before it happens? Where's the fun in that?

Clichéd though it is, life really is about the journey. And the longer I work with this stuff, the less I believe that there even is a destination; I think perhaps the journey itself is the point of it all. Life is a *process*; an unfolding, like the petals of a flower; a becoming. And learning to understand and embrace this process is why we're here. We are here to become all that we can be, and following our own paths is the only way to do that.

You have something special to offer the world: your unique talent, your unique gift, your unique perspective. So what's holding you back? You don't need to be perfect. You just need to be you. You just need to find your own way to share your own gifts with the world, in whatever way feels right for you.

That's why you're here. You'll never have all the answers, but you don't have to know all the answers right now. You just need to take a risk and start moving in the direction of your dreams. The answers will come as they are needed.

The Greatest Risk

There is a poem by Janet Rand called "Risk" that I first read as a teenager. And there is a line in that poem that I have always remembered, and which has always stood out for me and it says: "The greatest risk in life is to risk nothing. The person who risks nothing does nothing, has nothing, is nothing, and becomes nothing."

The big problem with fear is that it so often acts as a paralytic. We become so focused on everything that could go wrong if we follow that path we want to, that we fail to move at all.

It's the classic case of the devil you know versus the devil you don't. We're afraid to risk the certainty of the known – *whether we're happy with it or not* – for the uncertainty of the unknown. So we cling to what is. We turn our lives into something we've *settled* for, and condemn ourselves to always wonder what would have happened... *if.*

THE ALLURE OF THE "IMPOSSIBLE DREAM"

This is something that is really well illustrated in *The Alchemist*, by Paulo Coelho – there is a passage in that book where the hero has been working for a crystal merchant for some time and has made so much money for him that the merchant can finally afford his lifelong dream of going to Mecca. But the merchant tells the boy that he won't do it because holding onto his dream is what keeps him going and makes his life tolerable; he's afraid that if the dream is realized he'll have no reason to go on living.

At first I thought this was an absolutely ridiculous notion; how could the realization of a dream be anything but amazingly, incredibly, exhilaratingly awesome? But then it occurred to me that maybe, just maybe, the merchant had a point. Maybe, for some people, the greater risk is that if they go out and live that dream, it won't live up to their expectations and they still won't be happy. And so they hunker down in the misery that they know rather than risk the worse potential pain of a dream that wasn't what they hoped it would be.

HAPPINESS IS ALWAYS AN INSIDE JOB

But happiness is always an inside job – no thing, no situation, and no dream can bring us happiness – not unless and until we are already happy on our own. All those things and situations and dreams that we want will just add to that *pre-existing* happiness, but they don't magically *create* happiness for us. The key is to get happy *now*, while you're working on that dream, by using things like mindfulness and gratitude, and by giving yourself permission to *enjoy* living your life. That way, when your dreams do come true, they will just magnify the happiness that you've already *chosen* for yourself.

And if a dream doesn't live up to your expectations, well, that's not really a problem either, because there is always going to be a new dream! That's just part of life – as we change and grow and gain new experiences and understanding, our dreams evolve right along with us. So if you get somewhere and don't like it... *then change it!* Follow a new path or blaze a new trail -- that's what you're *supposed* to do! And in the process of getting to that first dream, you will have learned and experienced so many new things that the journey itself will have been worth the effort.

IS IT WORTH THE RISK?

We fear so much when it comes to our dreams, and yet we give up so much by not taking the risk to create the life we dream of, because when we give up on what our hearts truly want, we give up a piece of ourselves. And this is where we really do give up any chance we have for real happiness, because being happy comes from being true to Who We Really Are.

So the question becomes: is it worth the risk? Is it worth doing the things that scare the crap out of you in order to move yourself closer to your dream?

You are the only one who can make that choice. You can choose to avoid all risk and settle for a life that is half-lived, or you can choose to take the risk of venturing forth into the unknown and maybe creating something extraordinary in the process.

WHAT IF YOU WANT IT ALL?

As with Coelho's merchant, one of the things that I often hear from people is that they are really afraid to start moving towards their dream in case it turns out that it's not what they wanted after all. This is something that many people struggle with, and I think it all comes down to a mistaken belief that we have to choose one thing, over all others, to commit ourselves to for all eternity.

For those of us who have a great many interests and talents, choosing *just one* thing is indescribably painful; in fact, it's impossible. It can't be done. And there's the Catch-22: we've been brought up in a society that says we have to choose our One Path or One Career or One Field, and that we have to concentrate on that one thing and let everything else go if we're ever going to amount to anything and be "successful". We've been told that we need to concentrate and focus on becoming experts, even if that means pushing all the other things we loved to the side; even if it costs us our happiness.

But what if that's a false belief? Gone are the days when doing your best for the company that hired you meant that they, in turn, would take care of you until retirement and reward you with a gold watch after forty years of dedicated service. Over the last couple of decades, that hasn't been the scenario for many people at all. The working world has changed considerably, and in this new reality it is those who are able to adapt to rapidly changing landscapes who are best able to land on their feet – and those people are the ones with multiple skills and talents to draw from.

Beyond that, in my opinion, if you're not happy, you're not successful! Who decided on this whole "do one thing and one thing only" rule? It's utterly ridiculous. And if other people want to live by that rule, that's their business, but I see no reason why I, or anyone else, should have to if it doesn't work for us.

"But I Want to Be a Pirate!"

One day my son, who was five at the time, was moping about the house looking positively glum, so I asked him what was going on. And he looked at me so seriously, and he said "Mommy, I have a big problem."

I couldn't imagine what big problem a five-year old could possibly have that would be so serious, but I said "OK. Want to tell me what your big problem is?" And he said "I can't decide what I want to be when I grow up."

All I could think was: *You're FIVE; why are you worrying about this NOW?* But I said "What do you mean?" And he said "I want to be a pirate and a race car driver and a firefighter and an inventor and I don't know which one to choose." And he was actually *really* upset about this!

So I said "Hmm. Well, why do you need choose? Why can't you be all of those things?"

And he looked at me in surprise for a moment, and then his whole face just lit up and he said "You mean I can be ALL of them?!" And I said "Sure! Why not? Maybe you can be a pirate with an office on your ship where you invent things while you're sailing around the world, and maybe on weekends you can be a firefighter, and maybe you can be a race car driver for fun, when you feel like taking a break from sailing your pirate ship." And he was so happy, and so *relieved* by the thought that he didn't have to choose just one thing, that he could be *all* of them if that's what he really wanted.

THINK OUTSIDE THE BOX

Now, obviously there is a big difference between a five-year old not knowing what he wants to be and, say, a 49-year old not knowing what she wants to be. But the concept is the same. We get ourselves into this fearful mindset that says we have to choose, and it can only be one thing. And that's where we run into problems. Why choose? Why *not* do it all?

The only rules that say you have to choose come from outside *opinion*; there are no laws that tell you have to choose or you'll go to jail, for instance. There is nothing immoral or fundamentally wrong about NOT choosing. So why do we put ourselves into this box? Step out of the box! Don't make yourself choose just one of those precious jewels – those wonderful talents and interests — that you've been blessed with. You have them all for a *reason*. Trust that if they're in your heart, there is a way for all of them to happen for you.

Creating Your Awesome List

Here's what I want you to do: Take out your journal and get out that favourite pen. And then write a list of absolutely *everything* that you want to do or experience in your life, from the grandest, most extravagant, down to the smallest, most seemingly insignificant. Write it all down, so you have it saved and you know you won't forget any of those important dreams and goals. This is going to go a long way to alleviating that fear of missing out on something because all the things you want to do will be accounted for, acknowledged, and *validated*.

Now, some might call this a "bucket list", but I've never really liked that concept, myself. This whole idea of "do it now because someday you're gonna die" is not motivating for me. I prefer to concentrate on the whole concept of "Oh my goodness, I have this whole incredible, amazing, awesome life to live! What kinds of incredible, amazing things and experiences can I fill it up with?" So I have an "Awesome List" rather than a "Bucket List" and that's a much more motivating and energizing thought and focus for me. But pick whatever works for you.

Prioritizing: How to Do It All

Once you have your list, the next thing to do is to prioritize your items somewhat. If you're the kind of person who has many interests and goals, then you're going to have to get creative with your planning. You're not just planning for one career or possibility – you're creating a plan to encompass ALL the things you want to do. Realize that time is a constraint you'll have to deal with; you can absolutely do it all, but you may not be able to do it all this year, for instance.

Maybe this is the year you focus on photography and dog-training. And next year, you're going to take night courses at a culinary school while you set up your online business to sell all those awesome pictures you took this year, and on weekends you're going to hire yourself out as a magician for kids' parties. Be creative! Just because other people's schedules and lives are organized in one particular way does *not* mean that yours has to be the same.

NOT YOUR REGULAR 9 TO 5

If you have lots of different interests and goals you want to achieve, your life is not going to look the same as someone who has a regular 9 to 5 kind of existence.

If you want to be a photojournalist and document your trip through the desert, for example, but you also want to be a scuba instructor in Hawaii, your time is going to be organized a lot differently. Maybe you spend six months doing your photojournalism, and maybe even create a film documentary while you're at it (just for the fun of it), and then for the other six months of the year, you're teaching people how to scuba dive (and doing the post-production work on your desert life documentary during your off hours).

Or maybe what you want most is to become the next Stephen King, writing streams of best-selling, chart-topping horror novels. And while you do have a regular 9 to 5 job, you're diligently writing your manuscripts in the evenings, leading local ghost-walk tours on weekends, and spending your vacation time investigating the spookiest locations you can find for "background research" on your next series.

When you have many interests, you're going to have to plan further ahead than others. Where most people just plan for the coming year, you're going to have a fairly good idea of what you're going to be doing two years, five years, ten years, even twenty years down the road.

That doesn't mean that those long-term plans, goals and dreams can't change – expect that they *will* change as *you* change – but the point of those long-term plans is that you're going to know that all the things you want to do in life are accounted for. You don't need to choose, and there's no longer any need to fear that you're going to miss out on something, because you will know that you're going to get around to all of your dreams sooner or later.

BEEN THERE, DONE THAT!

This whole inability to choose and feeling like I was drifting aimlessly was something that I struggled with for years. My background and experience are all over the board. I have university degrees in both cognitive science and education. I like web design, I like teaching, I like curriculum design, I like psychology and I like philosophy. I want to get a publishing contract and write a best-seller. I love to cook and I want to write a recipe book. I love to sing and write music and I want to put an album together. I want to become a great motivational speaker. I want to go spend a month in England while still running my online business, and my kids love to go to the beach, so I'd love to take them for an extended stay in the Cayman Islands.

I have many, many interests, and many, many things that I'm very good at, and I love to keep busy and learn new things all the time. And with interests and talents that are as diverse as mine, I struggled for years trying to decide what I wanted to be and what I wanted to do. I have had numerous jobs, in many different fields.

I remember showing up for a job interview once and being asked to "explain my résumé" because I'd worked in so many different fields that they couldn't figure out what I did, or what box I fit in! I've worked with teachers, I've worked with trades, I've worked with lawyers, I've worked with doctors, and I've worked with PhDs. I've been a corporate trainer, a communications specialist, a web designer, a software support specialist, an educational technology consultant, a technical writer, a classroom teacher, a Human Resources specialist, and I've also been an executive assistant. You name it, and I've probably done it at one point or another!

GETTING OUT OF YOUR OWN WAY

I was never truly happy in any of those fields, however. And it wasn't until I understood that what I really wanted, and *needed*, was to do ALL the things that I loved, that I was able to start creating the kind of work-life experience that felt right. My biggest challenge in creating that kind of experience was doing the mental work of getting out of my own way and allowing myself to believe that it was OK to have a life that looked different than everyone else's.

But that's what I do now with my blog and coaching business. I use all my interests, passions and talents every day: My web background, my education and training background, my psychology background, even my crazy work history and oddly widespread experience; it all fits together perfectly in what I'm doing now. I just had to get creative and be open to all the different ways in which the things I wanted to do could manifest in my life, and not try to control or box things into structures that have been defined by outside opinion of how things *should* be.

So don't choose. You don't need to, and you don't need to worry about missing out on something that's important to you. Do it all. Be creative and find awesome new ways to make it all work for you, because if you want it all, you can absolutely have it all. Make your list, and start charting out your long-term plans. It will help you get yourself organized and give you that direction and structure that you're looking for, while making sure that all those things you want to do are acknowledged and accounted for.

DREAMS DON'T BUILD THEMSELVES

Once you know what you're dealing with, the next key is to take those first steps and get yourself started. Your dreams are not going to build themselves. You are going to have to start taking action, even when you don't know how it's going to turn out, and no matter how scared you are, if you ever want to see those dreams become a reality.

One of the quotes I have on my annual vision board is from author Karen Lamb, and it says "a year from now you'll wish you had started today". It's kind of a kick in the pants for me; a reminder to take consistent action towards making my dreams and goals a reality. It's so easy to get caught up in the trap of telling ourselves that we'll do it tomorrow or that we'll get to it later. But there's another quote out there, from 16th century Catholic priest Martin Luther, that says: "how soon *not now* becomes *never*".

The only way to get over your fear of the unknown is to start moving. Now. Today. You absolutely *must* start taking action if you want to get through this fear and get back on track to creating that extraordinary life that you envision for yourself. But don't worry; you don't have to take the cannonball approach to getting started if you're not comfortable with it; you can take the toe-dipping approach and start with baby steps instead!

YOU NEED A PLAN!

One of the best ways of getting yourself started on your action steps is to have a plan. Things don't always work out according to plan, of course, and you should make it a point to stay flexible about how your plans get executed. But it does help to have a good, general idea about where you're going, what you're going to do, and when.

As you learned in Chapter 5, most people have this romanticized notion of success being a straight line to the top, but the truth is that people take "wrong" turns all the time. Even successful people sometimes have no idea what they're doing; they just know that they have to keep moving and learning, and trying different things in order to achieve the kind of success they dream about. It's only when you look back and can see the view from the top that the path you ended up on kind of makes sense. As you're walking it, you often have no idea if it's going to work or not. You're pitching balls out to the Universe, or dropping multiple lines into the water, and hoping something is going result in a home run or a bite from "the big one".

CONSISTENT, INTENTIONAL ACTION

This does not mean that successful people just went out and randomly, haphazardly, did stuff without having a long-term goal in mind. Success rarely comes through blind luck and aimless wandering. It comes from actions that are done consistently, and with intent. You always know what you're trying to accomplish with your action; what you *don't* always know is whether it's actually going to give you the kind of results you're hoping for. But you're sending it out there to see. And when it doesn't work, you're not giving up; you're re-evaluating your strategy and thinking of something else to try.

When I first started getting serious about my blog and trying to build a business around it, I was a stay-at-home mother of two very young children, trying to cope with my father's terminal illness and subsequent death, and I was in a rocky marriage that was just about to end (although I didn't know that part at the time).

In short, I was exhausted and stressed out pretty much all the time. And when I would get to the point where I was completely wiped from looking after the little ones, trying to keep a house in order, coping with the ongoing marital tension, dealing with my own grief and stress, and trying to get a new enterprise off the ground, I had to remind myself that action was necessary in order to get to where I wanted to be.

The mountain wasn't going to come to me so if I wanted to see what was on the other side, I was going to have to start climbing, even though all I wanted to do was crawl into bed and sleep.

Aligning With Your Compass Point

Climbing that mountain had to start with some sort of plan; a roadmap and a strategy for how to get to the top. So, I made a list of all the things that I wanted to accomplish over the remainder of the year. It was kind of like a central repository of all the hopes and dreams that I had for myself, and it helped to keep me motivated and on track, like a compass point that kept me pointed in the right direction.

Ever since then, I've kept that list going, and at various points throughout the year I revisit my list: updating, adding, changing and, yes, even deleting things as my priorities and desires evolve. Over time, dreams can and do shift, so I actually *expect* to make changes to my list as each year rolls along; it's kind of like taking a moment to compare the paths marked on a map to the actual reality of the landscape around me and updating my route accordingly.

Mountain Climbing 101

I highly recommend setting up such a list for yourself to help keep you pointed in the right direction for your own dreams and goals. But an up-to-date list of dreams is just a list unless you actually DO something to make those dreams a reality for yourself. So what I suggest is that you prioritize your list of dreams, and then break them down into baby steps: smaller items or goals that will help you to achieve the larger dream.

The key is to start small. For example, I like to make lists of actionable items that I can do to make progress towards my goals, and then cross them off as I get them done. I love seeing a list full of crossed off items; it really gives me the feeling of having accomplished something because it's a very visual way for me to track my progress!

For example, when I first launched my blog, some of the action items were to:

- purchase URL
- set up web hosting
- install WordPress
- set up Facebook page
- write first article

These were all tiny little steps that didn't seem like much at the time, but all those tiny little steps that I took over the first four months turned into a full-fledged blog with almost 50 posts, over 2000 social media followers, growing numbers of RSS and newsletter subscribers, associated online gift shops, and a free eBook to help people make big changes in their lives. And that was just the stuff that was actually live; it didn't include the "in progress" things that I was working on behind the scenes!

All of this was accomplished in the span of only *four months* just by taking baby steps every day.

BABY STEPS ADD UP

By continuing my baby-steps approach and taking consistent action every day, I've since:

- grown my blog to over 400 free articles and videos;
- more than quadrupled my social media followers;
- racked up over one million views in Google+;
- launched my first online course
- self-published my first book on Amazon (it even hit #1 on one of Amazon's best-seller lists in Canada!);
- had my articles published in numerous places, including the *Huffington Post*, and on the web sites of three different best-selling authors; and,
- received an invitation to present with a big motivational speaking tour.

These are all little "wins" that are working together to help build the foundation for my bigger dreams.

MAKE ACTION A HABIT

Getting yourself into the habit of taking baby steps towards your goal every single day is *the* best way to start making things happen and to start making your own dreams come true. If you only do one single tiny thing to bring yourself closer to your goal, but you do one every day, that's 7 steps closer every week, 30 steps closer every month, and 365 steps closer in a year!

Likewise, if you only dedicate 15 minutes per day to your goal, but you consistently put that 15 minutes in every single day, you will have dedicated over 91 hours to making your biggest dream come true by the end of the year.

Baby steps add up to big progress, and each time you cross one of those action items off your list, it energizes you to keep going and do more! As your motivation builds and you start to see real evidence that you can do it – that you're *already* doing it – your fear of the unknown starts to fade because you have proof that you can handle whatever comes your way.

So go ahead... dream big! Then break it down into bite-sized, actionable steps. Commit to taking one little step towards your dream every day, and before you know it you'll be where you wanted to be.

Chapter 8 Recap

❖ **Key Points to Remember:**

- Fear of the unknown is at the heart of all the other fears. Everything comes down to a fear of not knowing what's going to happen next.
- You will never have all the answers, but you don't need them in order to start taking action and making progress.
- The greatest risk you can take in life is to take no risks.
- You don't have to choose just One Thing to do forever; you really can do it all, as long as you plan accordingly and are open to thinking outside the box when it comes to what your life and schedule will look like.
- Small action steps, taken consistently, are the key to massive progress and long-term success.

❖ **Your Action Items:**

1. Create your Awesome List; make a list of everything that you would like to do or experience in life.
2. Prioritize the items in your Awesome List and draft a plan that takes into account what you're going to focus on over the next 1, 5 and 10 years.
3. Pick one of the Awesome List items that you're focusing on this year and start breaking it down into smaller milestones and action items that you can start working on today.

❖ **Your Action Items:**

- http://www.VibeShifting.com/fearless-bonus

Chapter 9: Strategies for FearLESSness

> LIFE BEGINS WHERE FEAR ENDS.
> ~Osho, Indian Mystic and Spiritual Teacher

So now you know what your fears are, where they come from, how they're interfering with your ability to create a life you really love, and why you absolutely need to get through them if you're ever going to successfully turn your biggest dreams into reality. You've even learned some specific strategies for dealing with the four main dream-killing fears that people tend to struggle with. You also understand that, although you will never get rid of your fears altogether, you can learn how reduce them and fear *less*.

What I'd like to do now is break out the "big guns" and give you the heavy-duty strategies that are going to help you with that fearLESSness: I want you to have some core techniques for reducing fear in all areas of your life. These strategies build on all the others that you've learned so far, and help you take them to the next level; they are the real keys to setting yourself up for lifelong success and an extraordinary life lived on your own terms.

Up until this chapter, all our strategies for coping with fear have been more or less action-based. But now it's time to go beyond the surface and look inside, because the most powerful methods for dissolving fear are those that work with your own thought processes, beliefs, and expectations. As you learned in Chapter 3, your thoughts affect your emotions and your beliefs, your emotions and your beliefs affect your actions, and your actions create your reality. In a very real way, what happens in the world outside of you is directly shaped by what's going on inside your own mind.

And the first strategy for making the mental shifts necessary for a rock-solid dream-building foundation is to get clear on your "why" – the very personal reasons and touchstones at the very heart of your dream.

THE POWER OF WHY

"Why" is such a tiny little word, but it's such a compelling one. It's one of the first words we learn, and the one we use the most often as children because it's the one that allows us to learn the most about the world we live in and our place within it. It's only after years of listening to big people tell us to stop asking so many questions that we stop asking "why?"

And it's unfortunate, because when it comes to our biggest dreams in life, knowing our *why* is critical to figuring out our *how* and creating our *when*. "Why" is the foundation for moving our dreams out of the realm of fantasy and into our physical reality.

I once posted a blog article about never giving up on your dreams and about how our greatest breakthroughs often come just at the moment of our greatest despair. Which is all true; but how do you get yourself through that despair in order to get to the breakthrough? When your energy is gone and you're drained and exhausted, and what you've been doing isn't getting you the results you thought it would, and you have no idea what to do next, and you're feeling like maybe everyone was right after all and maybe it really is too hard... how can you possibly drag yourself back to your feet and keep going?

You can if you know your "why" – the reason and the meaning behind what it is that you're trying to accomplish or achieve. Because there is *always* a reason; whatever it is that we want to do, have, or become in life, there is always a greater reason behind the desire itself. Reconnecting with that reason reconnects you with your core values and beliefs and the very purpose for which you are here; *this* is the power of why.

YOUR "WHY" IS YOUR ANCHOR

Nineteenth century German philosopher Friedrich Nietzsche once said that "he who has a *why* to live can bear almost any *how*". Knowing and understanding why your dream is important to you – the underlying reason for doing what you're doing – gives you something solid to hold onto when things get difficult. And make no mistake about that; when you're trying to build a big dream, there *will* be times when things get difficult.

We are all here to learn things and I think that part of the reason our dreams are so important to us and why they will never let us rest, no matter how diligently we try to silence them, is because those dreams hold our greatest potential for personal growth. Creating the vision we hold for ourselves within our biggest dreams is the best possible way for us to become all that we are capable of becoming, and to contribute all that we are capable of contributing to this world and to the expansion of all that is. And that kind of a journey – the journey of discovering the real you – is *going* to be bumpy in places; it is going to stretch you out of your comfort zone. And when the fear and self-doubt are strongest, it is the power of your personal *why* that will keep you going.

If you know why something is important to you it, it gives you clarity, focus and direction of purpose. Once you make the decision to start moving towards your dream, things often start to happen fairly quickly. Sometimes, it can seem like a bit of a whirlwind as avenues open up and options start lining up for you. And it's easy to get sidetracked, distracted, or just completely overwhelmed by everything that seems to happening all at once. When this happens, your why will be the compass point that leads you back to your best path and keeps you going in the right direction.

Your why is the fire that burns within you; it fuels your determination and it inspires and motivates you to keep working towards that grand vision that you have for yourself. It's the energy source that will pull you back to your feet when you get knocked down by circumstance, or when you make mistakes. It's the voice within you, pushing you to ever-greater heights and telling you that *you must do this.*

In short, the power of *why* is the force that allows you to get through whatever it takes in order to get yourself to where you want to be. It is your anchor, your direction and your motivation to succeed. Your *why* is what allows you to work through your resistance, create your vision, and live your dream. You MUST figure out your why in order to get through your fears!

FINDING YOUR TOUCHSTONES

When my father passed away, I was handed some file folders and asked to untangle some of the aspects of his estate, and I came across some papers that were misfiled in those folders. The papers were my father's annual goals and objectives.

I only had a couple of those documents, but they were dated decades apart, so I think he'd been creating them for the better part of his adult life. And what I read in those documents made me realize even more, just how special my dad really was. Because written at the very top of each of those pages, before he went into the details and specifics about what he wanted to accomplish during the year, was this:

> **"The principle purpose of my life is to make the world a better place".**

I had no idea that my dad had these annual goals and objectives that he reviewed every year, but reading through these documents made me realize that everything he did – the entire way he lived his life – was based on this main objective of wanting to make the world a better place, and it made me even prouder to be his daughter. This guiding principle – this *touchstone* – that was so carefully printed at the top of these documents was my father's *why*.

What's Really Important to You?

If you're having trouble coming up with your *why*, refer to your first exercise from Chapter 1; think about what you will gain from making your dream a reality, and what will it cost you if you don't, and see if you can find a general "why" within your answers. Then flesh it out with what you've just learned above by finding your touchstones; the standards, guiding principles or fundamental truths by which you want to live your life. What is the foundation upon which you want to base your reasons for doing the things you do?

The key to this exercise is to let go of what you think *should* be your touchstones – let go of all the expectations, and connect with what's really important to *you*.

One of the hardest, but greatest, things that any of us can learn is to let go of the programming we've picked up from the world and the people around us. We try so hard to mold ourselves to fit into those expectations because we want so much to please, and yet this kind of situation never makes anyone happy; not us, and not the ones we're trying to please, because we can never *truly* become something that we're not. It takes a lot of courage to choose to let all that go and be who you are and who *you* want to be, instead.

Breaking Negative Thought Habits

Another mental strategy for overcoming fear is to become aware of your "little negatives" and put a stop to them. One of the things I frequently talk about on my blog is the idea of clearing up negative thought habits and replacing them with healthier and more productive thoughts, on the premise that when we change our thoughts we change our world. And one of the most effective ways of doing this is to get rid of all the draining negative thought habits that we've accumulated over the years.

WHAT ARE "LITTLE NEGATIVES"?

"Little negatives" is a term coined by American author and clergyman Norman Vincent Peale in his book *The Power of Positive Thinking*. Little negatives are the small negative thoughts that clutter up our minds and pepper our conversations. They are the worry words that we unconsciously inject into our thoughts and phrases throughout our day, such as:

- "I hope we're not late."
- "What if there's traffic?"
- "What if it rains? I hope I don't forget my umbrella."
- "I'm never going to finish in time; there's too much to do!"
- "There are so many applicants I'll never get the job."

Taken one-by-one, they're not such a big deal (they are "little", after all). The problem, however, arises when all these little negatives get added up. Taken over the course of a day, and by extension, over the course of weeks, months, years, and a lifetime, all these little negatives add up to a really big negative attitude overall. More importantly, they condition our subconscious minds into seeing everything through negativity-coloured glasses, casting shadows over every aspect of our lives without us even being aware of the damage they're doing (remember the Reticular Activating System from Chapter 1?)

CULTIVATING BEAUTIFUL DREAMS

Think of your subconscious mind as the soil in which you cultivate everything that you're going to grow or build in your life, and you can get a better understanding of how important it is to weed out these little negatives before they can take root and choke out the dreams and goals that you're trying to achieve.

If you want your flowers to be healthy, you have to give them good soil, feed them and water them. The same is true of your dreams; if you really want to manifest them into your life, you have to give them a good medium to grow in and you have to feed them and water them with positivity and thoughts of success. A mind full of negative thoughts is not conducive to growing beautiful dreams!

HOW TO WEED OUT YOUR "LITTLE NEGATIVES"

Fortunately, weeding out the little negatives is just a matter of shifting your ingrained thought patterns. Start by making it a point to monitor your thoughts and conversations for the little negatives that you, personally, tend to use. You'll start to notice patterns in your little negatives; there will be specific ones that you tend to use more often than others, and you'll start to notice the types of situations that tend to trigger your negative thoughts more than others.

Once you are aware of these patterns and the negative thoughts you've been automatically defaulting to, it will be easier for you to stop yourself from using them. Over time, you'll even be able to head off the "usual" negative thoughts before they surface.

For example, when you realize that you've made a negative comment or found a worrying thought such as: "There are so many applicants, I'll never get in!" floating through your mind, deliberately tell yourself to stop. Reframe the comment or thought into something more positive, such as: "Wow! If so many people are applying for this job, then it must be an awesome place to work!" and then say it out loud or think it to yourself. With enough practice, this reframing will become automatic and your thoughts will become naturally more positive.

We all deal with negative thoughts running wild in our heads sometimes, but if we take the time and make it our intent to overcome these little negatives, we ease the fear-inducing inner dialogue that makes us doubt our own ability to succeed and that, in turn, makes it so much easier to move forward with our dreams and goals.

RESISTANCE IS *NOT* FUTILE

In Chapter 1, you learned that one of the things you can expect to encounter as you start making progress toward your biggest dreams is *resistance.*

Understanding resistance and how it works is critical to being able to move through your fears and keep moving forward with those dreams because, despite what the all-conquering Borg species in *Star Trek: The Next Generation* would have you believe, resistance is *not* futile. In fact, resistance is a defining characteristic of all of four of the dream-killing fears that we've talked about in this book. Resistance is a force that will do its utmost to prevent you from ever achieving your goals and turning your biggest dreams into reality. It's the whole package of thoughts and feelings within you that are contrary to what it is that you say you want; all the unconscious *stuff* that's holding you back from really committing yourself, on a core level, to what you're trying to create.

If you let it, resistance will suck your soul dry and leave you mired in the hell that is the almost-but-not-quite. In short, it's the thing that chains you to unrealized potential.

The Master of Disguise

Resistance tells us that not going after the dream is the most reasonable thing to do and it gives us all sorts of excellent reasons why we shouldn't. And it is such a clever beast – it's a master of disguise and can cloak itself in ways that make its seductive words seem like the most sane and logical course of action we could take.

But all its words and reasons are outright lies. Resistance is not here to protect you, or help you in any way. Its sole *raison d'être* is the destruction of your dream; the utter waste of that special gift that only you can bring to this world. They say the road to hell is paved with good intentions... well, resistance is the one who built that road in the first place.

As you learned in Chapter 1, when you lose your dream – when you give up on it or let it go — you are dooming yourself to a lifetime of wondering what would have happened... *if*. If you'd been brave enough. If you'd been determined enough. If you'd been strong enough. If you'd been motivated enough. If you'd just stood up for yourself and taken the chance to make it happen.

The Biggest Cause of Misery

The thing is, there is nothing more harmful to the human soul than *not* going after the dream. This is the biggest cause of misery and unhappiness out there. When you are not actively becoming the best version of you that you can be... it destroys you from the inside out. Resistance may be slowly crushing your dreams, but they will *never* die completely; they are too much a part of you.

Even when you try to let them go they will continue to gnaw at you forever. No matter what you do or where you go, they will be calling to you, desperately trying to turn you in the right direction. And there is nowhere in all of Creation that you can run or hide that will keep those dreams from whispering to you... *begging* you to turn them into a reality. And this is why resistance is so dangerous. The sole purpose of resistance is to prevent you from taking the action that is necessary to succeed.

It will appeal to your sense of responsibility; it will guilt-trip you; it will seduce you by telling you that you will be happier if you just let it go. It will tell you that it's too hard. It will tell you that another option would make more sense for you. It will tell you that putting things off is the best way to make things happen. It will tell you *anything* it needs to tell you in order keep you from doing what you must do in order to turn your dreams into reality.

Where Does Resistance Come From?

In order to understand where your particular resistance is coming from, you have to look at the *whole* picture behind what you're trying to manifest. We touched on this a little bit in Chapter 6; in the case of manifesting huge piles of money, for example, most people think about the "wouldn't it be fab to be freaking rich?" aspect of things, but they don't think about what comes with all that money, at least not on a conscious level.

It's all percolating around in the recesses of their minds, however. So, somewhere inside of them, the thought of suddenly becoming incredibly wealthy is generating thoughts such as:

- I have no idea how to look after tons of money. What if I lose it all just as quickly as I gain it?
- What if people treat me differently if I'm rich?
- What if everyone I know starts asking me for money? If I give some to everyone, there'll be nothing left for me. But if I don't give it away, everyone will think I'm a horrible person.
- What if Crazy Uncle George wants me to invest in one of his harebrained schemes? How do I say no without causing a family war?
- Would this make tax time even *more* complicated?

Again, as we discussed in Chapter 6, a big change, like suddenly getting lots of money in your life, doesn't happen in isolation. It's not just your money situation that will be different; there are ripple effects to changes like that which affect every aspect of your life. Even if you haven't deliberately taken those other aspects into consideration, rest assured that your diligent little subconscious mind certainly has.

And while you're daydreaming about your future yacht, there is a part of you that, at the same time, is hyper-focused on all the negative effects of your desire, instead. And all those below-the-surface negative thoughts then add up to tip the scales in favour of *not* manifesting that desire or achieving that goal.

WHAT RESISTANCE TELLS YOU

Resistance, you see, *knows* you. In some ways, it knows you better than you know yourself. It knows how to manipulate you, and it will not hesitate to do so. It knows exactly what to tell you to make you procrastinate and put things off, and it knows how to make you think that that is actually a good thing.

You'll be squashing your dreams and thinking you're doing the right thing by doing so, even though you're destroying a part of yourself in the process. And the really insidious thing about it all is that the more important that dream of yours is to you, the stronger your resistance to actually making it happen will be.

It's critical that you recognize resistance when it crops up, for two reasons:

1. Obviously, it should be a danger signal to you that you need to be very careful about what messages you're listening to and acting upon; and
2. It should also be a signal to you that you are on the right path; when you're feeling resistance towards doing something that you *know* will help you, it is a sign that this is the direction in which you absolutely *must* move forward.

Seeing resistance for what it really is will help you to harness it in a way that will actually *help* you to achieve what you want to. If you are *aware* that resistance has reared its ugly head, you can then use it as a catalyst to propel you forward. But the first thing you need to do is figure out how to recognize it when it's there.

How to Identify Resistance

In order to identify any resistance issues you may have around a particular dream or goal, try this exercise:

STEP 1: IMAGINE YOUR SUCCESS

Sit quietly and imagine yourself in the already manifested situation, as if your desired outcome has already happened; you've already got the money, or landed the job, or met "the one".

STEP 2: IMAGINE THE OUTCOMES

Now imagine *all* the effects that this will have in your life (remember that nothing happens in isolation!). Think of both the big things and the small things.

STEP 3: FILL IN THE DETAILS

How does the manifestation of your desire affect your daily life? What are you eating? Doing? Where are you living? How do you spend your days? How are the people around you reacting? Try to imagine these things as realistically as possible – don't catastrophize things, but don't gloss over things, either. Make a list of everything you can think of.

If you *know* that you have a specific fear that might be holding you back from manifesting what you want, be sure to write it down as well, in your own words.

Once you've made your list, take some time to review it. The happy things or good changes that you think would come about through your manifestation are the things that you want to put on your vision board and what you want to concentrate on when you visualize. The negative things are the ones that are holding you back. These are the fears that are messing with your ability to follow through and create what you want. These are the resistance issues you need to work on and eliminate in order to move ahead.

How to Eliminate Resistance

Once you have identified your personal form of resistance, the key to eliminating it is to understand that there is nothing outside of you that causes it. Resistance is purely psychological; completely an internal thing. It is fear caused by what you think *might* happen.

This is so important so I'm going to say it again: *resistance is an internal struggle.* None of what you are worried about has actually happened in your real world; all of these fears are *hypothetical* and may never come to pass, but your thoughts about these "maybes" are strong enough to mess up your intentions.

In other words, it is not your Crazy Uncle George trying to get you involved in his harebrained schemes that is holding you back from your money; it is your own mind (you thinking about possibly being in that situation) that is holding you back.

Here are a couple of strategies that you can use to help you to get through those resistant thoughts and anxieties:

Strategy 1: See Your Fears for What They Really Are

Sometimes, identifying and bringing the fearful thoughts out into the open by writing them down like you just did in the previous section is enough to dispel them. When we bring fear out of the shadows and into the light of day, it often loses its power over us because we can see that it isn't as powerful as we thought it was.

As you learned in Chapter 8, when something is unseen or unknown our imaginations tend to build it up into something scary, but shining a light onto it lets us see it for what it really is.

STRATEGY 2: CREATE CONTINGENCY PLANS BEFORE ANYTHING HAPPENS

For the fears that still concern you, figure out how you can deal with them before they happen. For example: if you're concerned about how you're going to look after lots of money, then make a plan to hire an accountant and financial planner who can help you because, after all, if you have that much money you'll certainly be able to hire such help! Do some research and draw up a list of certified financial planners and tax accountants near you, and include their phone numbers and email addresses so you'll be prepared. Heck, why not research private banking options for the ultra-wealthy while you're at it!

And if you're still worried about Crazy Uncle George, then script it out. Write down what you think he's likely to say and then write down a good response that you can give him so you'll know how you're going to handle it before it ever happens.

Do this for each of the fears on your list – create a response script or a task list for every single one of them. Figure out how you're going to handle each fear and write it all down. Once you know how you're going to handle your fears – and more importantly, once you realize that *you are more than capable of handling those fears* – they will lose their power over you and stop interfering in your ability to build your dreams.

The Doorway to Your Dreams

Train yourself to see resistance as the doorway to everything you want in life. Don't go looking for it, of course, but when you notice it cropping up, realize that it is a neon sign pointing the way to the course of action that will be most beneficial to your own personal evolution or emergence. When you feel resistance, it means that *this* is what you need to do in order to get to your next level.

So do it.

Recognize what the resistance is and what it means. Let it make you angry if that's what it takes – how dare resistance stand between you and everything you want most in life? How dare resistance try to tell you that this isn't what you really want when you can *feel* with every fibre of your being that *it is*? How dare resistance try to squash the precious gift that only you can give to this beautiful world? How dare it.

Fuel for the Fire

Let the realization that resistance is standing between you and your dream fuel your determination to succeed. Feel the power that comes with this realization and then use every single trick you know to get yourself through it. Just freaking *do it*! Got a book you want to write? Make yourself write every single day. Set a timer and focus yourself completely on getting it done. It doesn't matter if what you write is any good, as long as you make sure to write during the time you have dedicated to the task, and that you do it consistently.

Want to launch a business but keep putting things off? Same thing; use a timer and get things done. Just decide to do it and then make it happen. Whatever your dream is, commit yourself to taking real action towards it every single day despite anything in you that tries to convince you not to. Build that website. Sign up for the audition. Submit your demo tape. Apply for the job. Ask about showing your work at that new gallery. Just do *something* today to bring yourself closer to that dream. And then do something else to bring you even closer tomorrow.

Don't let resistance continue to crush your dreams. Don't let it drain your soul. See that resistance for the destructive force that it is and push through it. The only power it has is the power you give it. Take that power back and channel it into building that which you want most in life!

BECOMING CERTAIN

One of the catch-phrases of the late American self-help author Wayne Dyer was: "I'll see it when I believe it." And this, I have discovered, really is the fundamental, core truth that predicts the successful outcome of what you're trying to create. Becoming certain that what you want is *going* to happen is the ultimate key to manifesting success.

But what does this actually mean? It means that when you believe, at a fundamental, core level, that what you want *will* happen, that's usually the point at which it does. Your beliefs and expectations have to be completely aligned with that desire before it can materialize in your physical reality. It may not be right that instant, but it usually happens fairly quickly once you have that unshakeable certainty.

YOU JUST KNOW

It's not a zealousness thing – there's a calmness to it; a sense of implacable, inescapable finality to it. *It. Will. Happen.* There's no doubt, but there's also no sense of over-excitement, either. There is just a sense that it's a given, and you don't need to worry or fuss about it at all. In my own life, I have had many experiences with this phenomenon. Here are just a few:

- I just knew I was going to go to a particular university, even though I was being told it would make considerably more financial sense to go to one of the schools in town, instead. I got accepted into my program of choice, on my campus of choice, and I also managed to get jobs with the University during the school year, and great-paying summer-student jobs back home that paid my tuition and residence fees.
- I just knew that I was going to get a government job in the computer science field when I graduated with that first degree, even though I had no idea which department it would be in or who I'd be working for. I got hired three weeks after starting my job search, into a position that ended up introducing me to the world of the Internet and web design.
- I just knew I was going to go to teacher's college, years after finishing my first degree, even though I didn't have the faintest idea about how I was going to make it happen. I talked to a friend who was a teacher, and she was so excited about the prospect of me becoming a teacher that she walked me through the entire application process, telling me exactly what to expect and how to structure my application responses to what they were looking for. I was accepted into the program.

- I just knew we were going to buy a particular house, even though my fiancé at the time didn't think we'd be able to afford it and refused to even look at the listing because of that. Circumstances shifted around us and money came to us in completely unexpected ways to allow us to make the kind of down payment that would leave us with mortgage payments we were comfortable with. We bought the house.

When you believe that something you want is inevitable — when you *really* believe it — that's when it tends to happen. Time and again, this phenomenon has been proven to me.

Clicking the "Print" Button

But why is certainty so important? Because it sends a signal out into the Universe that THIS IS. It's like sending a wireless signal to a printer; once the request to print has been sent, you don't worry about it and wonder if it's going to work – you just *know* that it *will*. So you don't even bother thinking about it anymore, really. Once that request is made, it's just a matter of waiting for it to actually print out.

All the tools and techniques that we like to use to help us stay focused on what we want to build in our lives – the visualizations and affirmations and scripting exercises – all of these tools are really just designed to program our minds to come to this conclusion, this *certainty,* that what we want is inevitable. It's *all* about becoming certain.

Chapter 9 Recap

❖ **KEY POINTS TO REMEMBER:**

- Your *why* is your anchor, your compass point, and your focus. Your *why* fuels your determination to succeed.
- Your touchstones are the guiding principles, or core values, that are most important to you in life. They will help you to find your *why*.
- Clearing up your habit of "little negatives" is critical to creating the right kind of mindset for success.
- Resistance is the whole package of thoughts and feelings within you that are contrary to what you say you want. It is the biggest obstacle standing between you and your dreams.
- When you believe at a fundamental, core level, that what you want will happen, that's usually the point at which it does.

❖ **YOUR ACTION ITEMS:**

1. Write down your touchstones – the core values and guiding principles by which you would like to live your life.
2. Review your first action exercise from Chapter 1. How do your touchstones fit in with these answers? Using both your touchstones and your Chapter 1 exercise, create one or two sentences to capture your *why*.

Chapter 9 Recap

❖ *Your Action Items (Cont'd):*

3. Pay attention to your personal "little negatives" and start to take deliberate action to stop them when they crop up. Reframe them into more positive thoughts to start training your mind (and your Reticular Activating System!) to start paying attention to the positive and helpful things in life.
4. Complete the exercise for identifying resistance on page 176, and then use the strategies for eliminating resistance on page 177 to create a response script or task list for coping with each of the fears you identify.

❖ *Download:*

- http://www.VibeShifting.com/fearless-bonus

Chapter 10: The Other Side of Fear

> SOMETIMES THE SMALLEST STEP IN THE RIGHT DIRECTION
> ENDS UP BEING THE BIGGEST STEP OF YOUR LIFE.
> TIP TOE IF YOU MUST, BUT TAKE THE STEP.
> ~Anonymous

In Chapter 8, we talked about how the greatest risk we can take in life is to choose to take no risks at all. When we avoid all risks, living our lives in fear of something going wrong, or in fear of not being capable of our ambitions, we end up not living our lives at all.

Fear is a powerful thing, and it causes so many of us to abandon the hopes and dreams that we hold most dear. When our own doubts are pounding at the doors of our hearts, we become susceptible to all the unsolicited advice of those around us who tell us to forget it; that the road we travel is too hard; that the odds are against us; that we are irresponsible for putting our dreams ahead of other's feelings;

that we need to face reality, forget our dreams, and just do what everyone else does.

In reality, an authentic life – a life lived boldly, fearlessly and fully – is not the easiest of options available to you. It's far easier to take the well-travelled safe route and live the life that you are expected to live. But if that's not making you happy, then maybe it's time to reconsider the usual. Maybe it's time to consider a different path and a different life; a life in which you become everything that you *know* you can be.

THE WHISPER WITHIN

There's always an element of risk in making life changes, in crafting a vision and building a dream. Taking something out of the realm of fantasy and turning it into reality requires thinking and acting differently than you have done in the past. It requires looking past everything you've been taught, ignoring what everyone else does or tells you to do, and trusting that little whisper within that tells you it's time to expand and grow. And it requires a certain amount of bravery and daring to do that. You must be willing to face your biggest fears head-on in order to make your biggest dreams come true.

Most people won't do it. Most people will not choose to face their fears because complacency is so much easier. It takes effort and determination, and the will to look within in order to first identify, and then work through those fears. It's so much easier to just turn away from that fire within you, to choose the simpler path, and to let the dream go.

Even if it Scares You

If you picked this book up, however, it's because that fire inside of you is burning stronger than anything outside of you that makes you think about giving up; it's because you've decided that you're not prepared to give up on your dream and live a life of "should" and "ought to". On some level, you have an intuitive understanding of how big of an impact your fears are having on your ability to make that dream of yours happens, and you're finally ready to do something about it.

You're finally ready to face those fears and take those first small steps toward everything you've ever wanted because you finally understand that if you want something in your life to change then you have to change the way you approach it; you have to think a little differently, act a little differently and just BE a little differently... even if it scares you.

Why Be Different?

If you keep doing and thinking what everyone else does, then you're going to continue getting what everyone else has. You have to be willing to move out of your comfort zone if you're going to build your dream. You have to risk being seen and attracting attention, and that's really hard for a lot of people. There is safety in being just another one of the flock, after all. But you're not a sheep; you're a uniquely talented individual with a wealth of experience, insight and strengths. And it's time to bring those gifts out and share them with the world. It's time to let yourself shine and embrace the idea of being different.

Change can be frightening; we can't know exactly what will happen when we set forth into the unknown. And doubts can be powerful, frightening things that make us question everything about ourselves, our decisions and our dreams themselves. But part of the journey of life is being open to the experience of it all. Even when circumstances seem worst, there is a balance in all things; where there is pain, there is the strength to endure it; where there is doubt, there is faith to overcome it; and where there is fear, there is love to dissolve it. As long as you don't give up, you will always get to the other side of it all.

THE MAGIC OF POSSIBILITY

Following your heart and following your dreams isn't always going to be easy. This is especially true when you've got all sorts of other "stuff" going on in your life. It's hard to keep yourself going when it seems like everything is going against you. But the mountains you think you see in front of you are mostly in your mind. Once you start climbing, you realize that they're not as big as you thought they were. There is no problem in life that is insurmountable, and if you can keep yourself focused on that vision of what you're trying to build with your life, it makes it easier to get through everything else.

When you make it a point to start acting, thinking and being different, you're giving yourself permission to explore. You're pushing the boundaries of that that safe little comfort zone you've created for yourself and expanding your horizons. You're giving yourself the gift of the unknown, the unusual, and the unexpected. And anything can happen. There is a world of endless possibility before you.

I love that word: "possibility". There's a magic to that, you know. You can feel it. And it's up to each and every one of us to take the *potential* of possibility and transform it into *reality*. And we can start doing that by making it a point to take full advantage of every opportunity that comes our way.

Making the Most of Opportunity

When you make the decision, once and for all, to go after that dream of yours with everything you've got, you're going to be shocked by how quickly things start happening. Opportunities really will start falling out of the sky for you, and sometimes they'll happen in the strangest of ways – but it's up to you to reach out and grab them. Opportunities, in and of themselves, mean nothing until you *do* something with them; they require a catalyst in order to amount to anything, and that catalyst is always action.

In order to be able to take advantage of incoming opportunities, it helps to be deliberately on the alert for them whenever and however they might present themselves to you. Be sure to keep both your mind and your eyes open because opportunities aren't usually announced with flashing neon signs and marching bands; more often they are understated little nudges, subtly pointing you in the right direction. They're found in the little synchronicities and coincidences that are the Universe's way of quietly communicating new avenues of possibility to you.

For example, when I first started to think about the possibility of writing guest posts for web sites other than my own, I started getting indications that it really was time for me to start branching out into that new-for-me area; articles about how to write and pitch guest posts started cropping up in my social media and RSS feeds, and in the span of two days, the leader of one of my networking groups sent out an email about opening up her own web site to guest writers, and I had a friend tell me that anytime I wanted to write a guest post for him, to let him know. Synchronicity. Coincidence. Message received. (And articles submitted!)

Trust Your Inner Guidance

When you get a flash of inspiration, trust it and run with it, even if it sounds crazy to you. I used to run a jewellery design business, and had all the usual social media sites for it, but the only people who really knew about that business were previous customers.

One day I just had a random thought that I should figure out how to get interviewed on the local television morning show, which was part of a larger national network. It really was a crazy idea — I was a tiny little one-woman hobby business selling handmade jewellery and, while I did have an "angle" to pitch, I figured that I was probably way too small for this show to have any interest in me. But I went to the show's web site and submitted a form anyway. I got an email that afternoon, asking if I could be available for an interview the next morning.

Sir Richard Branson, English billionaire and the founder of the Virgin Group, has a wonderful quote: "If somebody offers you an amazing opportunity but you are not sure you can do it, say yes – then learn how to do it later!" I love this quote because it's a reminder not to let fear dictate your path even if you are unsure about your ability to do something; if a golden opportunity floats your way, grab onto it and don't let your fear scare you away.

If you have a big dream, then you have to learn how to hit the ground running and be willing to learn new things all the time. Figuring out how to do something you don't currently know how to do is just par for the course, and if you can shift the way you look at that constant learning curve, it even becomes part of the excitement, adventure, and fun of building something incredible, rather than something to be afraid of.

Gifts from the Universe

Opportunity is always out there, and learning how to recognize it when it comes will help you to make the most of it. When we trust our instincts and follow our passions, the Universe seems to go out of its way to line up little surprises, coincidences and synchronicities for us. It's almost as if the consciousness that underlies all things delights in hiding little gifts for us, as guideposts to let us know that we are definitely following the right path.

When I wanted to start offering online e-courses through my web site, for example, I didn't have the technical set-up that was necessary for running that kind of learning environment, so I had to pick a software system that then needed to be installed and configured before I could launch my little "university".

I had no idea where to even begin and was quite daunted by the prospect of even attempting it (not to mention that I *really* didn't want to break the rest of my site in the process!) So what I concentrated on was what I was able to do at the time: building my first course, creating the content, and getting it all ready to go.

Then, shortly into my curriculum development process, I got an email from the business coach I had at the time (who did *not* do techy stuff for people). He said that he had actually been wanting to create a set of video tutorials for his own audience that would show them how to install and configure the exact software system I had chosen, and he offered to set the whole thing up for me if I would agree to letting him record the process while using my site for his demo videos! Problem solved, before it even became a real problem!

Becoming a Master of Synchronicity

This type of experience is so universal that I've even come up with a name for it - I call it the "Master of Synchronicity" process, and it's so easy to harness the power of this phenomenon to create manifesting miracles in all of our lives.

So how does it work? I've found there are only three things that we ever really need to do to master this process and get into the flow of it: 1) decide what we want; 2) start moving towards it; and 3) look for "magical" synchronicities and jump on them!

Step 1: Decide What You Want

The first step in becoming a Master of Synchronicity, and the cornerstone of the entire process, is to decide what it is that you want.

Get absolutely clear on what your goal really is and then *commit* yourself to making it happen. Because, as we learned in Chapter 3, there is a difference between committing yourself to what you want and just being "kind of interested" in it.

It's the difference between *becoming* a great piano player and just *wishing* you were great piano player, for example. Wishing might get you "Chopsticks", but only commitment will result in Mozart concertos. You will only take the action necessary to become a great piano player if you're committed to the idea, rather than just being interested in it.

STEP 2: START MOVING TOWARD IT

The second step is to start moving toward what you want: start taking action, in any way that you can, in the direction of that goal or vision. When you've made a choice to commit yourself to your vision, you'll find yourself getting all sorts of spontaneous ideas about things that you *could* do. When you get those ideas, follow up on them and *start doing!* You'll be surprised at how much progress you can make, in crazy-short amounts of time, when action is inspired in this way.

As you learned in Chapter 3, when you're working with inspired action you'll be working harder than you ever have before, but it won't feel like work because you'll be in that zone where everything is just flowing and you're filled with energy and enthusiasm for what you're doing. When you feel that energy and drive to do something, this is how you can tell that you're working with something you're truly passionate about!

STEP 3: LOOK FOR SYNCHRONICITIES

The third step is to look for golden opportunities and "magical" synchronicities. Once you start actively working towards a vision or goal that you've committed yourself to, things just seem to start lining up to make it happen for you, as if by magic.

These little synchronicities often come at you out of nowhere, and in the strangest ways; they may come in the form of overheard conversations giving you leads on something critical to your project, or just the right book showing up at just the right time, or someone you barely know may learn about what you're doing and offer up a key piece of information or a contact that will get you exactly what you need.

Seemingly random, serendipitous events will start to happen as you start moving forward. When these opportunities present themselves, jump on them! They are your signals from the Universe that you're doing exactly what it is that you need to be doing in order to get to where you want to be.

Becoming a Master of Synchronicity will help you to recognize and harness the power of those golden opportunities that come your way so you can start using them to turbo-charge your dream-building action steps!

Chapter 10 Recap

- ❖ *Key Points to Remember:*
  - If you want an extraordinary life, you have to be willing to go beyond the ordinary with your thoughts and your actions.
  - Most people will not make their dreams a reality because complacency is easier than facing your fears and doing the real work of building those dreams.
  - Opportunity usually presents itself in subtle ways; be on the lookout for it whenever and however it might appear.
  - When you get a flash of inspiration about a potential course of action, run with it!

- ❖ *Your Action Items:*
  - Review the Master of Synchronicity process on page 192; write down a specific milestone or goal that will get you closer to your dream.
  - Figure out smaller actions steps that you can take to achieve that milestone and do one *right now*. Start moving towards it!
  - Keep your eyes and ears open for magical synchronicities – overheard conversations, posters in coffee shops, random emails, etc. that provide you with additional information and missing puzzle pieces to help you with what you're trying to do.

- ❖ *Download:*
  - http://www.VibeShifting.com/fearless-bonus

Chapter 11:
A Life Less Ordinary

> OUR DEEPEST FEARS ARE LIKE DRAGONS
> GUARDING OUR GREATEST TREASURE.
> ~Rainer Maria Rilke, Austrian Poet and Novelist

Once you know exactly what's standing between you and everything you've ever wanted; once you understand that every single thing that is worth having in life and every single thing that really *matters* in life is found on the other side of your *fear*, you simultaneously gain the ability to overcome that fear.

If something is important to you, it's *going* to be scary; that's just the way it is. Whether it's a relationship, a business idea, a move to a new country, or whatever, every big dream comes with a price and that price is the fear you have to overcome in order to get what it is that you want.

Once you understand this simple truth, you can choose to start moving through the fear toward everything that you've been dreaming of.

A Commitment to Yourself

Making that choice is a big step, and it's a commitment to a different kind of mindset than most people have. It's a commitment to a different kind of existence. But most of all, it's a commitment to yourself; to the best that is within you.

When you have a big dream beating within your heart, giving it up out of fear and giving in to other people's *should's* and *ought to's* involves losing a part of yourself. When you feel called to a life that is different from the norm, it's not something that you can easily ignore or suppress, no matter how much other people might want you to.

Not everyone has a dream that strong. But for those that do, it becomes a part of *who you are*, and you can't just let that go – the dream simply will not allow it. If you have a dream like that, then you're different. You have always been different, and you will always be different.

The Road Less Travelled

If you have a dream like that, your path will lead you in a different direction than everyone you know, and you have to be willing to do something different than everyone you know in order to reach your goal.

Doing what everyone else does, thinking the way everyone else does, and talking about what everyone else talks about can only get you what everyone else has. If you want a life less ordinary — if you ever want to take that dream of yours out of your head and start *living* it — then you have to *do* something beyond the ordinary; you have to be willing to risk going off-road and seeking that which lies beyond your biggest fears.

Is it easy? Hell no. Your faith will be tested. Your courage will be tested. Your resolve will be tested. You're breaking new ground, going places few people dare go. You'll get flak from every side, and you will encounter resistance. You will be questioned and you will be tested in just about every conceivable way. You will doubt yourself and your choices, and some days you may even doubt your own sanity.

The initial steps along the road less travelled are not for the faint-hearted; it's hard to keep working towards a dream when you are uncertain of yourself and are afraid of making mistakes. It's even harder to continue forward into the unknown when everyone else around you seems to be so certain that you should be doing something else. It's so much easier to let the hysterical shouts from outside of you override the quiet, steady, voice that whispers within you.

"Everything You Want is This Way"

But the more you condition yourself to face your fears, the easier it becomes. One of the best things you will ever do for yourself is to start viewing your fears as a blatant, larger-than-life sign saying "everything you want is this way".

Make it a point to do something that scares you every single day — send those emails, or make those cold-calls, for instance — and you will start building up your fear-conquering muscles. And the further down that path you travel, the easier it becomes to tune out the noise from the rest of the world.

You Don't Have to Quit Your Day Job

You don't have to quit your day job to start building your dream. And it's not something I advise unless you're certain that's the route you really want to take. But there's nothing wrong with working both ends to the middle; keep the 9-5, but make a *commitment* that you *will* build that dream of yours with whatever time and whatever means you have available to you. Baby steps, remember. The mindset shift that comes with a clear commitment, combined with deliberate action towards your larger goal will start shifting your world in ways you cannot even begin to imagine right now. But you have to make the decision to start.

YOUR NEXT CHAPTER

You stand today at the start of a new chapter in your life. Today is the day that you make your decision: the easy route, or the one that might lead you to your biggest dreams. The safe route or the one that requires you to face every fear you have and find ways to move through them all.

Today is the day you decide which direction you're going to go, and one day, you may look back upon this moment as the turning point that changed everything for you. Because if you've read this far, I'm betting that I already know which path you're going to choose.

Yours is the path of the dreamer and the innovator. It is the path of fear and of risk, but it is also the path of adventure and infinite rewards.

Remember that behind every advance that humanity has ever seen is someone who overcame their fears and changed the world. Remember that every great achievement in this world started out as *somebody's* dream. Somebody had a dream in their heart, somebody was told it would never happen, somebody was terribly afraid, somebody was plagued by overwhelming self-doubt... but that somebody stood up to those fears and did it anyway. **Be that somebody**. Learn to fear less, and change your world.

Choose to be extraordinary...

Acknowledgements

Writing a book is a long process, and there are so many people who have had a part in making this particular book a reality.

Thank you, first of all, to my infinitely patient blog readers and newsletter subscribers who have been listening to me talk about "the new book" for well over a year now. You are the reason this book is here. You're the ones who share your stories, your hopes, and your dreams with me and who inspire me to continue writing. I am honoured and humbled to be a part of your life, in the small form of my words.

I would also like to express my deepest gratitude to two individuals who generously took time out of their very busy schedules to read early versions of this book and share their feedback. Without them, this book would not be what it is today: Kimberly Morand and David Perry.

Kim: you are a warrior queen with the heart of a poet. You are such an inspiration, both to me and to the thousands of women around the world who also read your blog. Your strength, your empathy, your wicked sense of humour, and your ability to share your vulnerabilities to help others heal are truly amazing. You keep me going when times get tough. In short, you rock, lady!

Dave: thank you for your insights, mentorship, and generous advice throughout this process. Thank you also for putting up with my endless avalanche of newbie-author questions with unparalleled grace, patience, and good humour; you really do have a heart of gold. You're the best cheering squad anyone could ever hope for, and you inspire me to keep working towards my own dreams, no matter what. You're one of the good guys, and I'm so glad we met.

Finally, and perhaps most importantly, I'd like to thank my children – my two beautiful little angels. You bring laughter, sunshine, and snuggles to my days and remind me what's really important in life. Always and forever, Mommy loves you.

Bonuses

Scan this code or visit the link below to grab your bonus resources, exclusively available to readers of *fearLESS*!

You'll get free access to a downloadable chapter-by-chapter workbook containing printable worksheets for the action exercises mentioned in each chapter, as well as infographics, cheat-sheets and templates!

www.VibeShifting.com/fearless-bonus

And don't forget to check out the *fearLESS* web site for even more goodies, including: videos, podcasts, tweetables and shareable images!

www.fear-less-book.com

FIND YOUR FEARLESSNESS

GET INSPIRED

Get weekly inspiration delivered right to your inbox by joining Nathalie's newsletter at:
www.VibeShifting.com/signup

GET SUPPORT

Wish you had a group of like-minded people to help motivate you in your quest to fear less? Join Nathalie's Facebook tribe at: www.VibeShifting.com/fbgroup

GET GOING

Loved this book and want to take the next step toward building your biggest dreams? Check out Nathalie's coaching packages and courses at: www.VibeShifting.com

GET CONNECTED

www.fear-less-book.com
www.VibeShifting.com
www.Facebook.com/vibeshifting
www.Twitter.com/vibeshifting
www.Pinterest.com/vibeshifting
www.VibeShifting.com/google

About the Author

Nathalie Thompson wants to live in a world where coffee pots are never empty and everyone is living the extraordinary life of their dreams.

A dream-catching catalyst and motivational expert, she is the author of *fearLESS* and *Seven-Minute Stress Busters* and her articles have been featured on the *Huffington Post* and on the blogs of NYT best-selling inspirational authors Pam Grout and Mike Dooley.

When she's not coaching clients, speaking for groups, or madly scribbling away on her latest writing project, you can find Nathalie searching for her constantly misplaced coffee cup or binge-watching episodes of *Doctor Who*, *Orphan Black*, and *Once Upon a Time*.

Connect with her and start transforming *your* dreams into reality over at www.VibeShifting.com!

/vibeshifting   @vibeshifting

REFERENCES

[1] http://msa.medicine.iu.edu/msa-newsletters/20130404/typing-or-writing
[2] http://www.wisegeek.org/what-is-the-reticular-activating-system.htm
[3] http://www.britannica.com/EBchecked/topic/287907/information-theory/214958/Physiology
[4] http://www.quora.com/Does-the-mind-record-everything-that-comes-through-our-five-physical-senses
[5] Watch the speech on YouTube: https://youtu.be/V80-gPkpH6M
[6] Paraphrased from the lyrics to "Let it Go", written by R. Lopez & K. Anderson-Lopez, from the movie "Frozen"
[7] http://en.wikipedia.org/wiki/Leonard_Nimoy
[8] http://en.wikipedia.org/wiki/George_Lucas
[9] http://thebrain.mcgill.ca/flash/d/d_04/d_04_cr/d_04_cr_peu/d_04_cr_peu.html
[10] http://en.wikipedia.org/wiki/Amygdala_hijack
[11] http://www.forbes.com/2010/07/07/stress-brain-relaxation-forbes-woman-well-being-health.html
[12] http://en.wikipedia.org/wiki/Confirmation_bias
[13] http://www.youtube.com/VibeShifting
[14] http://www.pinterest.com/VibeShifting
[15] http://en.wikipedia.org/wiki/Dyson_(company)
[16] http://www.idolator.com/7589634/rachel-platten-interview-fight-song-debut-ep-video
[17] http://en.wikipedia.org/wiki/J._K._Rowling
[18] http://en.wikipedia.org/wiki/Perfectionism_(psychology)
[19] http://en.wikipedia.org/wiki/Wright_brothers

[20] http://en.wikipedia.org/wiki/Impostor_syndrome
[21] Spoor, J., and Kipling D. Williams. "The evolution of an ostracism detection system." The evolution of the social mind: Evolutionary psychology and social cognition (2007): 279-292.
[22] http://www.VibeShifting.com/fbgroup

VibeShifting.com
DREAM·BELIEVE·ACHIEVE